"God wants to transform our broken world with radical love and justice. Grace Ji-Sun Kim and Graham Hill show us practical, life-giving ways that the church can help God's will be done on earth as it is in heaven."

Jacqui Lewis, senior minister at Middle Collegiate Church

"*Healing Our Broken Humanity* isn't so much a banquet as it is a big tasting plate, introducing us to a rich set of practices, rooted in the missional, contemplative, and progressive traditions of the church. Kim and Hill have packed their short book with such a vast array of ideas, resources, and stories, the reader's appetite to learn more and put it all into practice is thoroughly piqued—a wonderful intro-duction to the field."

Michael Frost, author of *To Alter Your World* and *Surprise the World!*

"There are many books dealing with diversity and reconciliation. Of all those books, including my own, I believe *Healing Our Broken Humanity* is the most relevant, hands-on, how-to manual on the subject you will encounter! Grace and Graham draw you into practical application from the earliest pages and they never let go. Regardless of whether you have been seeking ways to do the gospel in the midst of present brokenness or have become somewhat jaded to the theorizing of it, *Healing Our Broken Humanity* will not disappoint. Written by two powerfully sea-soned and wise mentors, they have found the missing link on this subject that everyone and every church should read. *Healing Our Broken Humanity* lives up to its subtitle, *Practices for Revitalizing the Church and Renewing the World*, and what could be better than that?"

Randy S. Woodley, author of *Shalom and the Community of Creation: An Indigenous Vision*

"In these pages two voices that I respect harmonize beautifully to sing of what the church can be. Part road map for forming a community in the healing purposes of God, part primer on intersectional theology, part Bible study on how justice is at the center of following Jesus, this book is wholly about the practices that make us a people who live to-gether more like Jesus (and less like jerks)."

Jarrod McKenna, cofounder of the #LoveMakesAWay movement and #FirstHomeProject for refugees

"Kim and Hill have marvelously provided what the church needs today: a road map for ways Christians can contribute to the common good and accordingly aid in the transformation of the world. *Healing Our Broken Humanity* is biblically grounded, sensitive to context, and eminently practical, as each chapter ends with concrete suggestions for 'practices, challenges, and activities for small groups' to move all those who encounter their book to immediate action. I heartily commend this book to all justice-seeking Christians."

Grace Yia-Hei Kao, associate professor of ethics at Claremont School of Theology, codirector at Center for Sexuality, Gender, and Religion

"The reality of a broken humanity is fundamental to a Christian understanding of the world. The temptation would be to simply offer a diagnostic that is a litany of lament over a fallen world. In this text, Kim and Hill not only offer an appropriate analysis, but also a Christian justice ethic that engages a theological depth and breadth. They also offer practical, real-life ways to put these principles into practice. For those who seek to revitalize and renew an active Christian faith, this book offers not a simple how-to guide, but a genuine, deep, significant, practical resource for the church."

Soong-Chan Rah, professor of church growth and evangelism at North Park Theological Seminary, author of *Many Colors* and *The Next Evangelicalism*

"This book is a clarion call for all those who dream of a church that is whole, holy, and humble, a church that acknowledges its own failings and seeks justice, and a church that seeks to join those who hope for a better humanity. It will inspire those who eschew the pursuit of power so they may better amplify the voices of the powerless and those who believe in community. This is a superb, clear-eyed call for all of those who dream of a better church and world, to begin to work toward it, and draw strength from the transformative power of love. There can be no greater and more urgent work than this."

Julia Baird, presenter on the Drum, columnist for the *Sydney Morning Herald* and the *International New York Times*

"In *Healing Our Broken Humanity*, two authentic voices from two continents offer the Christian church practical reflections to renew our mission, lives, and world. This work touches on critical contemporary issues facing our communities, and offers individual and communal responses that make a difference."

Joel Edwards, advocacy director for Christian Solidarity Worldwide, London

"In this outstanding work—thought provoking, theologically sound, wonderfully practical, and comprehensive in scope—Grace Ji-Sun Kim and Graham Hill effectively synthesize and ultimately advance key tenets of varying mindsets and movements within the church today, all in pursuit of a common goal: disruptive innovation in the local church whereby it is repurposed and positioned to advance a credible witness of God's love for all people in an increasingly diverse, globally connected, painfully polarized, and cynical society. *Healing Our Broken Humanity* is a thorough guide and inclusive playbook for pastors and parishioners alike seeking to engage the complexities of race, class, culture, gender, politics, and more, in a biblically accurate and informed way, and in so doing recognize that such things as lament, corporate repentance, reconciliation, and justice are not peripheral but intrinsic to the gospel."

Mark DeYmaz, directional leader of Mosaic Church of Central Arkansas, president of Mosaix Global Network

"This marvelous book is a practical and relevant resource that will help the church work with God to build renewed communities based on the new humanity in Christ. It will empower Christians to deal with the problem of racism and all forms of injustice. This book emphasizes the importance of corporate expressions of pain, grief, repentance, and lament. This comes at a time when the world is faced with fresh upheavals of tensions and resurgence of racism, nationalism, and white supremacy. I commend this book to all pastors and churches that are looking to equip the saints to face the challenges of racism, misogyny, nationalism, tribalism, and any other form of injustice."

Ngwedla Paul Msiza, president of Baptist World Alliance, Pretoria, South Africa

"There are plenty of reasons to throw our hands up in the air and walk away from the church. If we're honest, many of us have experienced it as a neutered counterfeit to the life and community Jesus invited us to embody. In this book, Grace and Graham remind us who we have been called to be all along, a new humanity in Christ who actively participate in healing our broken world. Rich in theological thought and firmly rooted in tangible practice, they invite us to be liberated into a cross-shaped ministry that leads to the flourishing of all. This isn't a church-growth strategy; it's holy provocation guiding us onto a path of confession, repentance, and new life. May this book be read and lived!"

Jon Huckins, cofounding director of Global Immersion, author *of Mending the Divides: Creative Love in a Conflicted World*

"This book is simply incredible. Goodness. So needed. I can't wait to get this in our church bookstore. It is robust in theology, rich in ecclesiology, and practical in application. Grace Ji-Sun Kim and Graham Hill paint the glorious vision of the bride of Christ rooted in the grand narrative of Scripture. Grace and Graham brilliantly put feet on this so any local church can catch a vision for participation in the healing of broken humanity."

Tara Beth Leach, author of *Emboldened,* senior pastor at First Church of the Nazarene of Pasadena

HEALING OUR <mark>BROKEN</mark> HUMANITY

PRACTICES FOR REVITALIZING THE CHURCH AND RENEWING THE WORLD

GRACE JI-SUN KIM
AND GRAHAM HILL

FOREWORD BY WILLIE JAMES JENNINGS

IVP Books

An imprint of InterVarsity Press
Downers Grove, Illinois

InterVarsity Press
P.O. Box 1400, Downers Grove, IL 60515-1426
ivpress.com
email@ivpress.com

InterVarsity Press® is the book-publishing division of InterVarsity Christian Fellowship/USA®, a movement of students and faculty active on campus at hundreds of universities, colleges, and schools of nursing in the United States of America, and a member movement of the International Fellowship of Evangelical Students. For information about local and regional activities, visit intervarsity.org.

All Scripture quotations, unless otherwise indicated, are taken from The Holy Bible, New International Version®, NIV®. Copyright © 1973, 1978, 1984, 2011 by Biblica, Inc.™ Used by permission of Zondervan. All rights reserved worldwide. www.zondervan.com. The "NIV" and "New International Version" are trademarks registered in the United States Patent and Trademark Office by Biblica, Inc.™

While any stories in this book are true, some names and identifying information may have been changed to protect the privacy of individuals.

Cover design: Chris Tobias
Interior design: Jeanna Wiggins
Images: geometric paint: © agsandrew / Adobe Stock

ISBN 978-0-8308-4541-5 (print)
ISBN 978-0-8308-7416-3 (digital)

Printed in the United States of America ∞

InterVarsity Press is committed to ecological stewardship and to the conservation of natural resources in all our operations. This book was printed using sustainably sourced paper.

Library of Congress Cataloging-in-Publication Data

Names: Kim, Grace Ji-Sun, 1969- author.
Title: Healing our broken humanity : practices for revitalizing the church
   and renewing the world / Grace Ji-Sun Kim and Graham Hill.
Description: Downers Grove : InterVarsity Press, 2018. | Includes index. |
   Identifiers: LCCN 2018014461 (print) | LCCN 2018022329 (ebook) | ISBN
   9780830874163 (eBook) | ISBN 9780830845415 (pbk. : alk. paper)
Subjects: LCSH: Church renewal.
Classification: LCC BV600.3 (ebook) | LCC BV600.3 .K555 2018 (print) | DDC
   261.8—dc23
LC record available at https://lccn.loc.gov/2018014461

P   21   20   19   18   17   16   15   14   13   12   11   10   9   8   7   6

Y   35   34   33   32   31   30   29   28   27   26   25   24   23   22

To my family, who teach me what it means to be new in Christ:

my spouse, Perry, and my three children, Theodore, Elisabeth, and Joshua.

And to my very special friends:

Graham Hill, who continuously inspires me to become new in Christ,

and Donald K. McKim, who encourages me every step of the way.

GRACE JI-SUN KIM

To Grace Hope Park: I thank my God for you, and pray you'll

grow to love Jesus deeply. I pray you'll live a full life,

shaped around God's grace and hope.

To Felicity, Madison, Grace, and Dakotah:

I'm astonished by how much you love me, and so

thankful to be doing life together with you.

And to Grace Ji-Sun Kim: your friendship is dear to me,

and a source of inspiration.

GRAHAM HILL

CONTENTS

Foreword by Willie James Jennings   1

Introduction: Nine Practices That Heal
Our Broken Humanity   7

ONE   Reimagine Church   21

TWO   Renew Lament   41

THREE   Repent Together   56

FOUR   Relinquish Power   76

FIVE   Restore Justice   91

SIX   Reactivate Hospitality 108

SEVEN   Reinforce Agency 126

EIGHT   Reconcile Relationships 138

NINE   Recover Life Together 152

Epilogue: A Benediction and Prayer 175

Acknowledgments 177

Appendix One: Questions for Discussion
and Engagement 181

Appendix Two: The Nine Transforming Practices
Accountability Form 189

Appendix Three: Resources for Healing
Our Broken Humanity 190

Notes 193

Index 209

FOREWORD

WILLIE JAMES JENNINGS

My grace is sufficient for you, for my power is made perfect in weakness," says 2 Corinthians 12:9. These words spoken by the Lord to Paul capture both the dilemma of Christian existence and its promise. Our dilemma is our weakness. We, the disciples of Jesus, are weak in relation to worldly power, whether it be military power, or the power of nation-states, or the power of corporations. Indeed, we are always immersed in the flows of worldly power. As Jesus said, we are inescapably in the world (Jn 17:14-16) and subject to its chaotic winds—economic, military, social, and environmental. Yet we do not belong to this world. We are not children created or sustained by worldly power. We are created and sustained by the Word of God (Jn 1:1-4; 1 Jn 1:1-3). The strength we live and move by is of God's only child, Jesus, who through the Holy Spirit works in us to do God's good will.

Our dilemma is our weakness, but so too is it our promise. God works in and through our weakness. The condition of our weakness is the stage on which God elects to work to overcome despair and hopelessness and to bring life out of death. Weakness works. But weakness is not a divine ploy, a façade that God uses to operate in worldly power. Our weakness points to the very shape of creaturely life. We are created for deep and intimate communion with the divine life. God desires to fill us with God's own strong life, a strength that is the source of life and a triune life that is the source of strength.

Paul articulated for us a life turned toward, not away from, weakness, and thereby a life turned toward, not away from, oneness with Jesus Christ. Paul experienced his weakness under the harsh conditions of real-world discipleship to Jesus, wherein violence confronted him on every side—from the Roman Empire, to various Jewish communities who saw him as a threat to their very survival, to rival leaders within Christian communities in the form of super-apostles (as he called them), who challenged his theological vision and the orthodoxy of his teachings. His astounding statement that he is "content with weaknesses, insults, hardships, persecutions, and calamities for the sake of Christ; for whenever I am weak, then I am strong" (2 Cor 12:10 NRSV) could only be made by someone who has entered into the urgency of God's moment and has yielded body and soul to the Spirit of God.

Paul's witness of strength in weakness has never been fully received by the disciples of Jesus. Indeed, our temptation has always been to seek to overcome our weakness by contorting ourselves to receive worldly power. We are created to receive the strength of God, but too often we mutilate ourselves in order to receive a different kind of power, a power that only leads to death. This mutilation is at heart the legacy of modern Christian colonialism. Many Christians since the beginning of the colonial period in the fifteenth century have presented themselves as worldly power brokers, not only capable of handling its power but also eagerly willing to attain such power by any means necessary. Forming themselves into nations, intoxicated with their unprecedented control over indigenous peoples and their lands, they brought into the world the horrors of racial reasoning and racial identities, new and more virulent forms of patriarchy, death-dealing forms of sexuality and intimate life, and ways of seeing the planet that reduced our world to a giant bowl of commodities created for the sole purpose of extraction, manipulation, and consumption.

The authors of this book understand this history very well, and they also know that the only way to move forward from this legacy is by returning to Paul's good witness of strength in weakness. Is it possible to overcome the contortions of mind and body brought to us through colonial modernity and a church that has lusted after worldly power? Is it possible to draw us away from ways of life that fit us for the power that leads to death and toward life in God's strength? The answer is yes. This is not an easy answer but one that can only be offered in faith, hope, and love, and one that requires lives aimed at following Jesus. To follow Jesus brings us to the practices of faith that clarify who we are and who we belong to, and that show that while we are in this world we do not belong to this world.

Christians have always talked about the practices of the faith, of piety, of mercy, and of justice. It is not new news that in order to be real, Christian faith has to be a faith practiced, for as James reminds us, faith without works is dead faith (Jas 2:17-18). Indeed, faith alone does not distinguish us from the demons. They believe too! (Jas 2:19). Throughout the centuries and across the globe, this has been a point driven home in sermon, song, and exhortation. In recent years theologians and philosophers and a whole host of other Christian intellectuals have made a profound intellectual turn to practices as the way to understand the very character of theology, the point of theological ethics, and even simply a meaningful life. You would be hard pressed to find anyone in the theological academy or in Christian communities who is not in favor of emphasizing Christian practices and the importance of practice. But the problem with this focus on practices has been its blindness to the colonial world formed by *practicing* Christians.

Colonial settlers from the very beginning were practicing Christians. They practiced their faith fully and completely, with orthodox intention and execution. Their liturgies, their prayer lives, their almsgiving, their repentance, their building up, their tearing down, their singing in hope, and their dreaming in faith—all these practices of the faith existed, thrived in fact, in the formation of the colonial world such that we feel their effects to this moment. From our place in history we can look back at these Christians and claim we see the contradictions in their faith, a colonializing, slaveholding, earth-destroying faith, but that would be too easy a way out of the horror that gave rise to colonial modernity. Faithful Christian practice was part of colonial history and was made into the training ground for forming people fit for worldly power. But that is not the only story of faithful Christian practice. Many people of the old world and the new world formed faithful Christian practices that resisted colonial power. These were Christians, both colonial settlers and indigenous peoples, who resisted worldly power and sought to redirect the operations of the world toward the good in God. They shared together in the witness of Paul, of strength made manifest in weakness.

So we are the inheritors of a legacy of Christian practice; on the one side are Christian practices that form people to operate in worldly power, and on the other side are Christian practices that form people to live into their weakness and their journey in God's strength. Let me be clear: the difference is not one of occupation. The difference is not between those involved in politics, government, industry, business, entertainment, the academy, and a host of other fields and those who are not. The difference is not between those who carry an optimism into these fields of endeavor and those who look at all operations of the world with a cunning cynicism. Indeed, one of the foolish things that has plagued the contemporary turn to practices has been people who have tried to approach faithful Christian practices as an alternative set of operations of politics, government, industry, business, entertainment, the academy, and so forth. They take isolation as a goal of faith-fulness, an essential element of Christian identity, and a character-istic of witness. Their folly comes from their blindness to colonial history, which has irreversibly connected this world together through a fabric of commodity chains, ecological manipulation, and violence. More importantly, this approach does not yet grasp our weakness—we are in the world, but we don't belong to it.

The difference between Christian practices that form people to operate in worldly power and practices that form people to live in the strength of the Spirit of God through their weakness is a difference not of quality, or consistency, or even knowledge, but of community. Faithful Christian practices today that follow Jesus are practices done in and among diverse communities where the histories of colonial wounds are addressed. No Christian practice done inside segregationist ways of living and thinking will draw us into our true strength in God. This was the fundamental flaw born of colonial Christian practice, a vision of Christian life comfortably separated along lines of gender, race, land ownership and land dispossession, national affiliation, neo-tribal designation, and money.

Kim and Hill in this courageous book are not simply offering us another account of Christian practices, but Christian practices that necessitate diverse communities for their performance. *The crucial matter today for Christian discipleship is not what you practice but who you practice with.* Who is present in our confession and repentance, in our lamenting and our justice work, in our offering hospitality and renouncing power? Whose stories, voices, wisdom, authority, guidance are missing when we gather to do church? Who is not present in giving shape to our prayers and praise, our advocacy and proclamation? Show me a Christian who sits comfortably in segregated ecclesial life, in a homogeneity of Christian practice, and I will show you someone who is formed for worldly power, that is, someone whose work in the world, in whatever endeavor they have chosen, always bends toward maintaining the status quo of segregation, of white supremacy, of Western imperialism, of the propagation of violence, and of the destruction of the planet.

Harsh words, yes, but true nonetheless, because there is no other option for Christians engaged in the practices of our faith. Either we are being formed toward worldly power or we are being formed toward our strength-in-weakness with God; either we are moving toward faithful practices that deform faith or faithful practices that actual form faith in God. It may seem strange to use the designation of "faithful" for deformed faith, but in truth there is an integrity to Christian practices even done under the conditions of colonial power, patriarchy, white supremacy, Western imperialism, and planetary destruction. Yet the integrity, consistency, and orthodoxy of Christian practices have never been enough to actually make them Christian. What makes them Christian is Jesus, following him into the lives of people different from us, drawing us through the Holy Spirit into that crowd of pleading people looking for help and release from the bondages of this world.

Too many people today are abandoning the church and imagining other spiritual practices that can heal themselves and the world. There is something good to be said about learning from the traditions of spiritual life beyond Christianity. But the tragedy in the efforts of too many is that they have never understood the great riches and overwhelming joy of Christian practices that touch the heart of Jesus and join us through the Holy Spirit to the world. Too many people have never learned how the church is not a door to shut out the world but a door to enter more deeply into its beating heart. If through our practices we follow Jesus into the depths of the world, then we will learn that the healing we all seek for ourselves and our world is offered to us not in our own strength but in God's power, if only we would seek it together.

INTRODUCTION

NINE PRACTICES THAT HEAL
OUR BROKEN HUMANITY

O n July 17, 2014, Eric Garner died after a police officer put him in a chokehold for almost nineteen seconds while arresting him. Garner was a forty-three-year-old African American man. He was wrestled to the ground by four police officers on suspicion of selling single cigarettes from packs without tax stamps. While one officer put his arm around Garner's neck, three others pinned him to the ground. Garner repeated "I can't breathe" eleven times while lying facedown on the pavement. He then lost consciousness, and the officers did not perform CPR at the scene. Garner died that day due to the brutality of his arrest.

In 2015 Ta-Nehisi Coates wrote a public letter to his son. In it he writes, "Here is what I would like for you to know. In America, it is tradition to destroy the black body—*it is heritage.*"[1] He then asked readers of *The Atlantic* to share their stories of racial prejudice. Many stories of racism and its consequences poured in. These are personal stories of racism, and public accounts of the brokenness of humanity.

We are living in a broken world. Western societies are struggling with the rise of racism, misogyny, nationalism, conflict, violence, and more. Many African Americans, Native Americans, Latinx, Asian Americans, and other minoritized groups think that systems are unjust.[2] Political, judicial, policing, and other systems seem stacked against them. Hundreds of thousands of people are displaced globally due to poverty, discrimination, climate change, or political and religious upheaval. They seek refuge, hope, freedom, and a new life.

Many political and public figures are making the most of these turbulent times. They appeal to xenophobia, nationalism, and antagonisms. These messages have been magnetic in parts of North America, Europe, Australia, and other settings. The conditions seem ripe to support racism, misogyny, exclusion, injustice, conflict, and division. Nations and peoples that once enjoyed unrivaled global power and influence now feel like they are in decline, and they don't know what to do about it.

A large percentage of the population feels disenfranchised from political and other systems that seem to support wealthy individuals and institutions. These systems seem deaf to them. They feel anxious, worried about the future, angry, and disoriented. They see themselves getting poorer. They see their neighborhoods becoming racially and religiously diverse. So they are looking for others to blame. Muslims, "foreigners," or undocumented immigrants are easy scapegoats. Societies that have been told how to speak about race, gender, and religion haven't really changed. They've just pushed these feelings and animosities down deeper, resulting in collective anger, prejudice, and fear.

Unfortunately, many Christian leaders and churches are going along with these currents. The church is no longer at the center of culture, power, economics, and politics, as it was in Christendom. Some Christian leaders are anxious about their waning influence. They worry about their loss of power and status. They're easy to woo because they want their chance in the spotlight and their access to power and the powerful. Various tribal allegiances too often form Christian identity. Confident, charismatic, successful, misogynistic, nationalistic, Christendom-courting, loudmouthed demagogues have filled the vacuum.

But here is the bright side! The church of Jesus Christ can speak life and hope into this situation. It can proclaim and embody the new creation in Christ, and show a different ethic and way of life in the world. God enables us, as God's one, new, and transformed people, to recover our humanity and help change the world. After all, we follow the one who goes into the storm saying, "Peace, be still."

The way the church embodies this new way of life in the world is its shared practices.

THE POWER OF PRACTICES

I (Graham) grew up in a suburb and family full of craftspeople and tradespeople. These were people skilled in a range of functional, decorative, or specialized crafts and trades. These included carpenters, tailors, stonemasons, builders, bricklayers, and electricians. It included floorers, landscapers, plumbers, roofers, welders, truck drivers, automotive mechanics, architects, and cabinetmakers. All plied their craft with skill. They made commitments to apprenticing one, two, or three others in their craft or trade. All honed their expertise. They saw their craft or trade in the light of the broader community of artisans. They worked together, building or renovating houses, sculpting landscapes, restoring automobiles, or fashioning garments or pieces of furniture.

The finished product was rarely the result of one craft or one artisan working alone. At times these tradespeople or craftspeople were only skilled in one area. But often they were multiskilled: carpenter-floorers, plumber-electricians, architect-landscapers, truckie-mechanics, or teacher-builder-electricians. My father restored houses from time to time—including my own house, after my wife, Felicity, and I moved to Sydney, Australia. When he did this he used an array of carpentry, electrical, plumbing, construction, architectural, roofing, flooring, and landscaping skills. And he called on the skills of others he trusted.

In that environment I learned the importance of discipline and practice, both personal and in community. A person becomes a highly skilled craftsperson or tradesperson (or dancer, musician, theologian, pastor, writer, etc.) through many years of hard work and personal discipline. This person, and the community the person is a part of, performs important, disciplined practices countless times, over many years. These practices form people personally, build the community's life together, and shape the fruit of people's lives and shared efforts. This is a community of discipline. It is a *practicing* community. These practices often lead to extraordinary and beautiful results.

I (Grace) have a teenage daughter, Elisabeth, who's an example of the power of disciplines and practices. Elisabeth has been taking ballet lessons since she was three years old. When she turned eight, her dance became more and more serious, and she had to focus and become a disciplined dancer. She goes to ballet four to seven days a week. When there are performances such as *The Nutcracker* or the spring dance, she is at her ballet studio for three to five hours per day to warm up, stretch, rehearse, and learn new routines. It takes skill to dance, but also lots and lots of practice to become a good dancer.

Elisabeth takes her classes and rehearsals very seriously. In class the dancers are not allowed to talk unless the instructor asks them a question. They are expected to quietly follow directions and practice new moves. There is a lot of repetition; the instructor makes them do movements over and over again until they have mastered them. The teacher points out what dancers are doing right or wrong and also uses a hands-on approach to lift or stretch their legs or arms properly. After hundreds of repetitions of the same movement, the students come to learn it.

Furthermore, after Elisabeth's dance classes and rehearsals, she comes home and does her homework and studies for her tests. Before bed she spends thirty minutes stretching and exercising. She is very careful about what she eats, doing her best to stay away from junk food and to eat fresh fruits and vegetables. She recognizes that a healthy body is needed to be a serious dancer.

Elisabeth's classes, routines, rehearsals, and healthy lifestyle are crucial to becoming a dancer. They have become part of her lifestyle, and they are all essential. The rest of us, whether we want to become a dancer or a faithful disciple of Christ, need to engage in similarly transforming practices.

Stanley Hauerwas says that formation happens in community.[3] This is because character is at the center of formation, and community forms character. Today we as Christians need to recover, as Hauerwas writes, "the integrity of the Christian community. Here is a community breaking out of the suffocating tyranny of American individualism in which each of us is made into his or her own tyrant. Here is an alternative people who exist, not because each of us made up his or her own mind but because we are *called*, called to submit our lives to the authority of the saints."[4] Hauerwas believes that we are called to submit ourselves to Christ and to a faithful community that practices its discipleship together.

In this community of character are individuals. They form an ethical life together and in the world through discipleship practices. These include Eucharist, simplicity, generosity, economic sharing, hospitality, creation care, reconciliation, peacemaking, and acts of justice. They include prayer, baptism, celebrating the liturgy, reading Scripture, fasting, serving with the mentally handicapped, and embracing asylum seekers, refugees, and undocumented neighbors. Importantly, they include immersing ourselves in the Gospels as the training manuals for Christian discipleship.

Formational practices need disciplined communities. But, as Hauerwas notes, shaping disciplined communities isn't easy. It's especially hard in modern, liberal-democratic, consumeristic, and individualistic societies. So much in these societies pushes back against discipline, accountability, stability, and community.[5] But discipleship and community must go hand in hand.[6]

Hauerwas draws on the metaphor of bricklaying. He says the church needs to learn to lay metaphorical bricks and to make disciples. Laying bricks involves "learning myriad skills, but also a language that forms and is formed by those skills."[7] It's about learning the craft from those who've gone before. It isn't primarily about gathering information. It's about discipline, training, craft, language, patience, character, and formation in community. This is how the church must make disciples. Discipleship involves learning a myriad of skills through personal discipline and by immersion in community. We also learn a language—words such as faith and hope and love take form in our mouths and shape our hearts and minds. And, so, discipleship practices and new ways of conceiving and speaking about God and the world shape our life together. Together, we learn fresh discipleship practices and vocabularies.

NINE TRANSFORMING PRACTICES

This book shows what it means to be the church, the new humanity in Jesus Christ, as Paul writes about in Ephesians 2:15. This is the biblical basis for our understanding of what it means to become new in Christ. The church shows the world God's perfect design for humanity, which is a reconciled, unified, whole, multiethnic, peaceful, loving life together. As a beacon to the world, the church shows the world what God calls it to be. The church shows the world its destiny and future. In an era where Christian identities seem so enmeshed with race, politics, nationalism, and material goods, we need to imagine a different reality.[8]

In *The Christian Imagination*, Willie James Jennings has shown how the Christian social imagination is often diseased and disfigured. It's wedded to racialized, individualistic, privatized, and rootless identities. We find ourselves in this place because of historical events. We need to confront this situation head-on and theologically if we are going to demonstrate a compelling witness and life together in the world. The church needs a compelling vision of a healed and whole Christian community (and a redeemed Christian social imagination). The church needs fresh practices before a watching world.

Too often our theological or intellectual posture is one of power and control. We expect others (e.g., indigenes, marginalized groups, and outsiders) to be adaptable, but we refuse to be so ourselves. In our attachment to power and control, rigidity, superiority, and staleness grow. This diseased posture stops Christians from forming habits of humility, fluidity, embodiment, and engagement, which lead to transformation. Yet, as Jennings says, we live in hope:

> Christianity marks the spot where, if noble dream joins hands with God-inspired hope and presses with great impatience against the insularities of life, for example, national, cultural, ethnic, economic, sexual, and racial, seeking the deeper ground upon which to seed a new way of belonging and living together, then we will find together not simply a new ground, not simply a new seed, but a life already prepared and offered to us.[9]

Race relations is one area where the church and Christianity can offer hope and a new way of life together. Race is a modern construct and problem, and such disciplines as biology, genetics, philosophy, history, political science, economics, feminism, cultural and post-colonial studies, and more are examining it. We need to understand "whiteness" and how whiteness is a construct to subordinate others. Yet, strangely, Christian theologians have been largely silent about race. A theological account of race is profoundly absent.

A few theologians and authors are seeking to fill this void. Willie James Jennings, Daniel Hill, Soong-Chan Rah, Christena Cleveland, Kwok Pui Lan, J. Kameron Carter, Drew G. I. Hart, Brenda Salter McNeil, Rick Richardson, Jim Wallis, Emmanuel Katongole, Ken Wytsma, Paula Harris, and Doug Schaupp are examples. They call the church to a new way of life together in the world in terms of race relations. This is a way of life characterized by justice, love, reconciliation, and peacemaking. These authors exemplify Christian hope for society in regard to this important topic.

This book unpacks what it means to be the new humanity in Christ, as we embrace nine transforming practices that we hope you can adopt into your life. The practices aren't necessarily sequential. You don't need to practice the fourth before you can go to the fifth, for example. These practices may be taking place concurrently, and different people might have different entry points.

1. *Reimagine church* as the new humanity in Jesus Christ.

2. *Renew lament* through corporate expressions of deep regret and sorrow.

3. *Repent together* of white cultural captivity, and racial and gender injustice, and of our complicity.

4. *Relinquish power* by giving up our own righteousness, status, privilege, selfish ambition, self-interests, vain conceit, and personal gain.

5. *Restore justice* to those who have been denied justice.

6. *Reactivate hospitality* by rejecting division and exclusion, and welcoming all kinds of people into the household of God.

7. *Reinforce agency* by supporting people's ability to make free, independent, and unfettered actions and choices.

8. *Reconcile relationships* through repentance, forgiveness, justice, and partnership.

9. *Recover life together* as a transformed community that lives out the vision of the Sermon on the Mount.

These nine practices enable us to be the new humanity in Jesus Christ. These nine practices transform the church and the world. They lead to reconciliation, justice, unity, peace, and love.

WHO WE ARE AND WHY WE ARE PASSIONATE ABOUT THIS BOOK

We want to take a moment to introduce ourselves and explain why we wrote this book. We've known each other for a few years now, since we first met when Graham did some filming with Grace for the GlobalChurch Project. Graham spent almost six months filming Asian, African, Latin American, indigenous, and diaspora Christian leaders about faith, witness, prayer, and more, and he caught up with Grace in New Jersey in early 2015 to do some filming with her on her writings. Over a couple of years, we shared stories about our passion for listening to the voices of minoritized people. We discovered a shared desire to invite often-unheard voices from around the world to enter into a powerful conversation about the shape of faith, reconciliation, and justice in the twenty-first century. In the process we became close friends and decided to write about these things together.

I (Graham) teach applied theology and world Christianity at Morling Theological College in Sydney, Australia. I'm the founding director of the GlobalChurch Project. I've been in Christian ministry since 1987, including church planting, pastoring local churches, and teaching at theological colleges. I'm passionate about the local church and about seeing neighborhoods and lives transformed.

I (Grace) am an associate professor of theology at Earlham School of Religion in Indiana, and I am an ordained Presbyterian Church (USA) minister. I have written several books on marginality, racism, sexism, and the need to embrace all people. As I grew up in Canada as a young immigrant child, it became very clear that my voice was often ignored. I experienced this firsthand in my elementary school. Because my first language isn't English, kids made fun of my accent every time I opened my mouth. This made me feel self-conscious about speaking out loud in the classroom. So even though I wanted to speak up and answer questions that the teacher was asking, I felt that I couldn't participate as I wanted, and as a result my voice became more and more silenced. In addition my voice was ignored in the Korean Presbyterian church that I grew up in. It was quite evident that male voices were welcomed, and women's voices were considered unimportant and a nuisance. The blatant silencing of women's voices was a painful reality for me and for other women in the church.

I (Graham) first became passionate about the transforming practices covered in this book in the late 1990s, when I was speaking at a conference in Manila in the Philippines. I was staying in a backpacker's hostel at night and speaking at conference sessions during the day. One morning I was woken by the sound of sobbing. I looked down from my bunk to see an elderly man weeping beside his bed. During the week I got to know this remarkable man. He was an elderly Vietnamese pastor who'd planted a church of a dozen people in his home thirty years earlier. That church had grown to tens of thousands of people. He told me stories from this Vietnamese church that sounded like something from the book of Acts. These were stories of miracles, lives transformed, persecution, and a growing, vibrant, underground church in communist Vietnam. But I noticed something. All the speakers at the conference in Manila looked like me: white men. So I started thinking about the injustice of this. Why weren't people like my elderly Vietnamese friend asked to speak, or at least to tell their stories? And I started wondering about the thousands and thousands of stories that are never heard: Christians whose voices are ignored, silenced, or marginalized. How do we start to hear these voices? How do we hear their cries for (and stories of) justice, peace, hope, and reconciliation? How do we learn from them and embrace new practices that can transform the world? That was the beginning of my journey, and these nine practices come out of listening to thousands of Christians from all over the world talk about the practices that they know can heal our broken world.

Our hope is that this book will be used by small groups, ministry professionals, activists, and laypeople. We hope this book will help you discover new, transforming practices that revitalize the church and its mission and that transform the world. We hope that through these nine practices you'll discover fresh expressions and depths of reconciliation, justice, unity, peace, and love.

HOW TO GET THE MOST OUT OF THIS BOOK

This book can be read individually, but we also believe it is helpful to read in community. We encourage you to read this book in your small group, as a ministry team, as a college class, or in some other group setting. You may choose to gather a group of friends and read this book together in a home or a coffee shop.

Here's how your group can get the most out of this book.

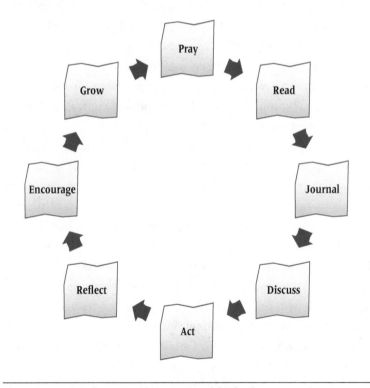

Figure 1. Practices for getting the most out of this book

Pray for open hearts. Spend time together in prayer and medi-
tation, asking God to prepare your hearts as you read the chapter
together. Ask the Spirit to make you open to what God wants to do in
your lives, group, church, and neighborhood. Ask God to give you an
open and receptive heart.

Read the chapter. Before your meeting, read through the chapter
for the week. Many of the chapters refer to Scripture too, so read with
your Bible open. Read slowly, reflectively, and prayerfully. Take your
time and allow the ideas and challenges to sink in. (If you are reading
this book together in your small group, you might choose to do one
practice per week over nine weeks, or two practices per week over
four weeks, and then one in a final week.)

Journal your thoughts. As you read the chapter, journal your
thoughts. Journal what God is saying to you. How is God asking you
to respond and change? What impresses or challenges you? What do
you agree or disagree with? What questions do you have? How is the
Spirit trying to get your attention and change your life? What is he
saying to your group, church, and neighborhood? How is God calling
you to think or act in response to your reading?

Discuss what you are learning. Meet in a small group or college
class, with some friends at home or at a coffee shop, or as part of a
ministry team. You will get a lot more out of this book when you read
it with others. Together you can think about the book's challenges
and implications. Discuss the chapter you read that week (or the two
chapters you read that week, if you've decided to work through this
book over five weeks). What are the key ideas? How does the chapter
invite your group to respond? What does the chapter mean for your
ministry, church, agency, family, or team? Appendix one has some
questions for discussion and application.

Act on the suggested practices and activities. At the end of every
chapter, there are three or more practices, challenges, and activities
for small groups. These will help you explore and apply the practice

discussed in that chapter and turn ideas into habits. Choose one of the suggested activities to do together that week. Set aside some time to do that activity together. (If an activity can't be completed that week, set aside some time in your calendar to do that activity later on. Some of the activities will take quite a few weeks to complete, so set aside some time to do that exercise this year.)

Reflect on what you are learning. As you do the small group practice or exercise together, talk through what you are learning. When you meet to read the next chapter, reflect together on what God is saying to you and how God wants you to respond personally and as a group. What did you learn and discover as you engaged in the small group activity together? Engage with each other's ideas. Listen and learn from each other's insights and experiences.

Encourage each other to change and grow. We all find it easier to change and grow when we are encouraged and supported. Find creative ways to encourage each other to pursue deeper discipleship and faith and to overcome old habits and prejudices. We encourage each other by (1) discerning together what God is saying to us, (2) spurring each other on to deeper faith, (3) challenging each other to change, (4) nurturing each other's faith, and (5) holding each other accountable.

Here's one way you can keep each other accountable. Appendix two has the "Nine Transforming Practices Accountability Form." Keep a copy of this form in your Bible or in your bag or journal.

Once a week, pull out this form and write some answers to the questions on the form.

Once a month, ask everyone in your group to pull out their forms, and then discuss each of the nine practices. Hold each other accountable for the commitments you make. This accountability will help you continue to change and grow.

Grow through further reading. It's important to keep growing and learning. Appendix three has resources for recovering our humanity. These are a few books on each of the nine practices that will help you learn more about the practice and how to apply it.

SMALL GROUP RESOURCES IN THIS BOOK

To help your group get the most out of this book, we've included the following four resources:

- *Small group activities* are proposed at the end of every chapter. These will help you apply the nine practices in your church and neighborhood.

- *Questions for discussion and application* are in appendix one. These will help you dig deeper into how to apply and understand each of the nine practices.

- *The Nine Transforming Practices Accountability Form* is in appendix two. This will help you keep each other accountable as you seek to live out the nine practices personally and together.

- *Resources for recovering our humanity* are offered in appendix three. These will help you to learn more about each of the practices and help you continue to grow.

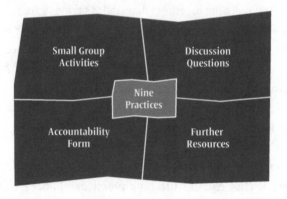

Figure 2. Resources in this book

With God's help, we can recover our humanity and pursue love, peace, justice, and reconciliation. These nine practices help encourage us to transform a dehumanized world into God's world.

ONE

REIMAGINE CHURCH

Jesus calls us to reimagine the church as the new humanity in Jesus Christ (Eph 2:15).

This is about learning together and anew about injustice and division in the church and the world. It's also about learning mutually and afresh what it means to be the new humanity in Jesus Christ.

WHAT IS "THE NEW HUMANITY IN CHRIST"?

As a child I (Graham) had the opportunity to visit the junction where the Darling and Murray Rivers meet and join in New South Wales, Australia. These are some of Australia's longest rivers. There's a viewing tower at the junction. A huge sign declares, "You are at the junction of Australia's Two Greatest Rivers." From the tower you can see the distinct difference between these two great rivers. Surrounded by majestic eucalyptus trees and the laughter of kookaburras, you look down on these rivers. The Darling River stretches 915 miles. It's a clay-based river and has a rich milky color. The Murray River is 1,558 miles long, and it flows through Australia's highest mountains all the way to the sea. It's a rich ecosystem of fish, turtles, shrimp, and platypuses, and it's a vibrant blue.

At the Darling and Murray Rivers junction, these two rivers become one great river. This is a stunning testimony to the God who creates, sustains, and restores all the heavens and the earth, and who makes the two into one.

What does Paul the apostle mean when he speaks of the new humanity in Christ?

Paul means that Jesus Christ has done away with the old divisions and enmities. He has united Jews and Gentiles as one new and undivided humanity in him through his death and resurrection. This is a new creation in Christ. God has made for Godself one new people out of the two. Christ has abolished the old divisions based on culture, politics, race, religion, law, gender, social standing, and so on. "Christ is all, and is in all" (Col 3:11) and has brought us together from every nation, language, and people as "one new people." This doesn't rid us of our Jewish or Gentile (or American, Korean, Australian, Chinese, Rwandan, Brazilian, Native American, etc.) cultures, identities, and unique contributions. But now our primary identity is in Christ and in that he has made us "one new humanity" in him (Eph 2:15; see Eph 2–4; Col 3; Gal 3; 6).

The political culture has become more polarized than ever in recent years. Sadly, many American Christians participated in this culture of divisiveness and animosity. Misunderstanding, accusations, and disunity continue in the church, even after the 2016 election. It's one thing to differ and engage in vigorous debate. But disunity, animosity, and division are another thing altogether.

Much of this division is rooted in our sense of personal and corporate identities. But Jesus calls us to shape new identities as the new humanity in Christ. This new identity forges new allegiances and new social imaginations. It nurtures a deep commitment to grace, forgiveness, and love. In a world full of division and conflict, the church needs to embrace the ministry of reconciliation and peacemaking. God calls us to be a peaceable people who display unity in diversity under Christ. God commands us to show the world what it means to be a new humanity and new creation in Christ.

So we are not primarily Tutsi or Hutu, German or French, British or Australian, Palestinian or Israeli, Chinese or Brazilian, Syrian or American. We are not primarily Republican or Democrat, conservative or progressive, urban or rural, rich or poor, white or a person of color. We bring all these identities and aspects of ourselves to our new humanity in Christ. We are primarily one people, united as one body in Jesus Christ. As a new creation and a new humanity, we are "a people on pilgrimage together, a mixed group, bearing witness to a new identity made possible by the Gospel."[1] God calls us to show the world what reconciled, redeemed, and restored humanity looks like.

We must not root Christian identity in nationalism, ethnicity, partisan politics, sociopolitical-economic status, gender, and other such things. Instead we must root Christian identity in discipleship to Jesus Christ. This identity is formed through a vision of what it means to be a distinct people with an alternative ethic, politic, and life together. That people, formed by God for Godself—Jew and Gentile, women and men, rich and poor, black and white—shows the world an alternative way. Together as a new humanity we are made up of every tribe and ethnicity and language, valuing difference and particularity but united in our Christian identity. This new people roots its story in Israel, in Jesus, and in a vision of the new humanity and the age to come, when God will rule and reign.

We Gentiles (Americans, Australians, British, Asians, Latin Americans, Africans, etc.) join the story of Jesus. Our particular histories and cultures (personal and group and ethnic) are still important. The story of Jesus gives some parts of those stories more and fresh meaning. And other parts are revealed as destructive or divisive. But, now, in Jesus Christ, all our personal and corporate stories are situated and framed within the story of biblical Israel, the Jewish Jesus, the new humanity, the new creation, and the age to come. We express this in grace, love, forgiveness, lament, fellowship, hospitality, welcome, and a commitment to human flourishing.

This unified identity is not the opposite of diversity. The church is intended to be diverse, and it has work to do in terms of becoming less monocultural and more intercultural. As Scot McKnight says, we are a "fellowship of differents." This means we understand Christian life as a fellowship, as a social revolution, as life together, and as transcending and honoring and enjoying difference. We understand Christian life "to be about love, justice, and reconciliation."[2] We must be a community of diverse races, languages, cultures, marital statuses, political views, genders, professions, experiences, ages, socioeconomic backgrounds, and much more.

It's not enough to talk about unity in diversity. Diversity without theological substance is shallow and secularized. We need a vision of *unity in diversity under Christ* that is rooted in Scripture and theology. This new humanity embraces distinct qualities and convictions.

THE QUALITIES AND CONVICTIONS OF NEW-HUMANITY CHURCHES

What are the qualities and convictions of new-humanity churches? These churches know that they are one body, with one Messiah, one Spirit, one life, one table, one politic, one righteousness, one peace, one mission, one faith, one hope, and one love. Let's unpack each of these.

One body. Jesus Christ calls his church to be one unified and diverse body. "Just as each of us has one body with many members, and these members do not all have the same function, so in Christ we, though many, form one body, and each member belongs to all the others" (Rom 12:4-5). As one body, our unity in diversity is under Christ and witnesses to him. It witnesses to his redemption and to his restorative future for all creation and humanity.

Too often diversity is co-opted by pragmatists for the sake of cultural relevance (or for "political correctness"). Too often diversity is just about reflecting the concerns or values of society. *Diversity* is often a code word for black and brown, which neglects Asians and Native Americans. But the church needs to do better than that. We must incarnate the value of diversity and implement it for biblical, theological, and missional reasons. We must build a theology of *unity in diversity under Christ* that shapes our life together and in the world. Bruce Milne writes:

> In today's context of in-your-face diversity, it is time to revisit the heart of the New Testament, with its claim that in Jesus Christ a new quality of human relationships has arrived and that the gathering of his followers in Christian churches represent a unique possibility of bridging the gulfs that separate.... Christian congregations, everywhere, are called to be just that— bridging-places, centers of reconciliation, where all the major diversities which separate human beings are overcome through the supernatural presence of the Holy Spirit.[3]

God's mission is to reach the whole world. Jesus poured out his Spirit at Pentecost on diverse peoples with diverse languages, traditions, hopes, cultures, and expectations (Acts 2). God works in and through racial, gender, linguistic, and generational diversity. God has given the gospel to all the nations, granting all peoples "repentance that leads to life" (Acts 11:18). In our unified diversity, we join with God in God's mission and welcome. This is the intercultural scope and embrace of the gospel. We reflect the extraordinary mosaic that emerges from God's hospitality and love (Acts 17:26-27).

God is reconciling the world in Jesus Christ. God is calling every ethnicity, and both women and men, to join in that ministry of reconciliation (2 Cor 5:14-21; Gal 3:28), to be a multiethnic and redemptive community that shows the world what the world looks like in its redeemed state. This community joins together in mission, ministry, worship, and community. God calls the church to be a light to a divided and broken world, to witness to the world as it breaks down the dividing walls of animosity, hatred, fear, and discrimination (Eph 2:11-22).

God is shaping the local and global church into the church of every nation, tribe, people, and language. One day we will all worship together as brothers and sisters before the throne of God (Rev 7:9-12). We seek to express this future in our life together today as we "put on the new self" (Col 3:10), both individually and corporately. Together we are renewed through the one in whom there is now no dividing distinctions, "but Christ is all, and is in all" (Col 3:11). Forgiveness, compassion, humility, kindness, gentleness, patience, justice, thankfulness, peace, worship, joy, and love, "which binds them all together in perfect unity" (Col 3:14), characterize our life together (see Col 3:1-17). We serve each other, caring for one another and honoring those whom the world may deem less honorable. Among God's people those who have been neglected, marginalized, silenced, forgotten, exploited, and broken are treated with dignity, honor, love, and respect (1 Cor 12:12-31).

As we embrace this theological, missional, and communal vision, we offer a compelling witness and life together in the world. We see this being lived out in churches around the world. When we think of New York City, we think of a cosmopolitan of diverse communities, ethnicities, and cultures. In that large city we can see a witness to life together in Riverside Church as different people from around the world worship and engage in ministry and life together. In Sunday morning worship there, you can see intercultural ministry being lived out as people of different walks of life come together to worship. The global church needs a compelling vision of a healed and whole Christian community like Riverside Church demonstrates. We need a redeemed Christian social imagination.[4] The global church needs fresh postures before a watching world.

Now, we need to be careful here. We'll never address racial injustice with tokenism, pragmatism, cultural accommodation, or window dressing. Merely replacing white male leaders and speakers with women and people of color won't solve any problems. In fact it'll just entrench problems. We need long-term, systemic, and theological solutions to animosity and division in the church and world.

That requires addressing the underlying issues. These include internalized racism and a diseased and disfigured Christian imagination. We need to get to the root of racialized, individualistic, privatized, and rootless identities. And we need to embrace and express a compelling, biblical vision of the church.

Only this way can we truly be the new humanity in Christ. Only this way can we truly be the church. Only this way can we have a strategic social ethic. Only this way can we show the world what God intends the world to be. Only this way can we embrace a compelling vision of a healed, whole, and multiethnic Christian community—one body in Jesus Christ.

One Messiah. Our unity comes from our Messiah, Jesus Christ. We are united with him in his death and resurrection as his body. He has created this new humanity and is the source and sustainer of our new life in him.

As Paul says, the Messiah is the image of the invisible God. He is the source of new and eternal life for all those who trust and believe in him, and he is the fullness of God. He reconciles humanity to God and to one another through his death and resurrection (Col 1:13-23). Any life, hope, vitality, forgiveness, and unity the church knows is only found in and through its Lord and Messiah. This is the ministry of reconciliation—between God and humanity, between whites and peoples of color, between rich and poor, between young and old, between Democrats and Republicans, between commerce and the earth, and the list goes on. Our reconciliation, redemption, and unity in diversity are in Christ alone. But let's not make any mistake—this is about justice, peace, freedom, reconciliation, and hope for all peoples and all creation. It goes beyond us. This is because everyone

and everything has "been created through him and for him. He is
before all things, and in him all things hold together. And he is the
head of the body, the church" (Col 1:16-18).

At one stage all who are Gentiles were "foreigners to the covenants
of the promise, without hope and without God in the world" (Eph
2:12). But now the Messiah has redeemed us by his blood, regardless
of our gender, age, language, culture, or race. He is our peace. He has
abolished division, enmity, conflict, fear, discrimination, and prejudice. He has made us one new people—a new humanity in Christ—
reconciling us to God and each other through the cross and abol-
ishing enmity. Together as one new people we are fellow citizens,
God's household, built on Christ Jesus and the prophets and apostles.
This new humanity is also a holy temple, again built on Jesus Christ,
the cornerstone, and "built together to become a dwelling in which
God lives by his Spirit" (Eph 2:22). How can we allow any disunity or
division to continue when the Messiah calls us to be reconciled and
unified in him?

One Spirit. The Messiah unifies a diverse church in the power of
his Spirit. The Spirit establishes, fills, empowers, and renews the
church as his ongoing and dynamic creation. The Spirit forms the
community into a countercultural community embodying the redemptive reign of God, helping it to be faithful, indwelling it with its
power and presence. The Spirit works in the church so that it is holy
and unified and gives it the ministry of reconciliation.

Jürgen Moltmann describes how the church enjoys "fellowship
with Christ" as the Spirit reveals Christ, unites the church with Christ,
glorifies Christ, and forms the church for the sake of Christ's messianic mission. "Faith in Christ and hope for the kingdom are due to
the presence of God in the Spirit."[5] The presence of the Spirit forms
the church as the "messianic fellowship of service for the kingdom of
God." And the Spirit helps the church see itself "as the messianic fellowship in the world and for the world."[6]

The Spirit creates the church and fills it with his grace. He empowers the church for the coming realm of God. The Spirit is present in and forms the church's sacraments, ministries, missions, and structures. Moreover, all these aspects of the church are "conceived in the movement and presence of the Spirit." The Spirit takes up the church's "gifts and the tasks assigned to it." The Spirit works in the church for the sake of the messianic mission and the eschatological realm of God.[7]

The church is one, holy, catholic, and apostolic in the power of the Spirit. And the Spirit uses these four attributes for the glory of Christ, for the unity of the church, and for the extension of the realm of God.[8] He works through them to bring liberation, healing, justice, mercy, and hope to a broken world.[9] In doing so the Spirit empowers the church to witness to divine love and reconciliation.[10] This is the work and fruit of the Spirit (Gal 5:22-26).

One life. The Messiah unifies and renews his church through *his* divine life. "I have come that they may have life, and have it to the full" (Jn 10:10). The Messiah doesn't just offer the church new life—he infuses the church with his very life-giving presence and power. People from every nation, tribe, and tongue join to receive this life, made one in the Messiah.

Colossians 2–3 contain warnings, promises, and commands. Persuasive arguments and empty ideologies are always trying to secure our allegiance and passions. These can be religious, political, cultural, or other types. But these are all empty deceptions that ensnare our hearts and lead to divisions, strife, and conflict among God's people. These ideologies split the church, leading to judgmentalism, idolatry, legalism, immorality, greed, division, pride, fear, and brokenness.

Instead Paul encourages us to lay hold of the Messiah, in whom all the fullness of God dwells in bodily form. In his life, death, resurrection, wisdom, and triumph is fullness of life. We have been buried and raised with him to new life—the full life only he can offer.

We are called by the Messiah to lay hold of that life together, as one body. This is "putting on the new self," personally and together, as a new people. Setting aside distinctions and divisions and empty arguments, we enter the fullness of life in God. We decide to live as a new humanity in which "Christ is all, and is in all" (Col 3:11).

This life is manifest as a new way of being in the world—one of compassion, humility, grace, holiness, and hope. "And over all these virtues put on love, which binds them all together in perfect unity" (Col 3:14).

One table. In Asian cultures, eating and sitting around the table is an act of welcome and hospitality. Sitting around the table is a vision of family, friends, and strangers coming together to share life together. The table is an important symbol of life, respect, and welcome. Traditionally in Korea, the table is usually low and round, and people sit on the floor around it. This means there is no need for chairs, so many people can gather around. If friends or strangers drop by, they are always welcome to sit at the table and join the meal. Furthermore, food is cut up into little pieces so that one can pick all of it up with chopsticks. There is no need for forks or knives to cut up the meat placed on one's plate. The act of cutting up food while cooking also allows for visitors to come in anytime to join a meal. This is in contrast to the West, where families often need to know exactly how many people are going to eat in order to prepare the exact number of pieces of steak or chicken per person.

In my (Grace) childhood in Korea, we all sat on the floor around the table. We always welcomed neighborhood kids and friends to drop by anytime to eat, as there was always room at the table. This is a powerful symbol of hospitality and embrace.

Ruth Padilla DeBorst says:

> Hospitality means conversion from individualism to community, from autonomy to interdependence, from idolatry to true worship, from grasping to receiving, from oppressive

dominion over creation to loving care of it, from indifference to passionate, prayerful action, from Western definitions of "development" to loving participation, from competition to collaboration, from protagonism to service.[11]

The new people that Jesus had in mind are a hospitable, welcoming, open, and generous people. We have responded to Jesus' welcome at the table, as we are recipients of Jesus' divine hospitality. We invite people of all nations, languages, cultures, and colors to our tables. We offer this hospitality to each other and to the world, sometimes while we ourselves are foreigners or displaced or sojourners. More often we welcome outsiders to our local culture.

When I was growing up as an immigrant in Canada, there seemed to be continual immigration from Korea. Every time a new immigrant family came to our neighborhood, my dad would invite them over. So we had strangers constantly coming to our home. When the Vietnam War broke out, there were lots of refugees; some people called them "boat people." When they came to Canada and into our neighborhood, our family opened our house to them. Friendships developed as we welcomed them and ate together and shared our stories of living in a new country.

Hospitality includes our relationship to our home, to the earth, and to a local place. It involves our connections to local relationships and local generosity. It includes the gifts that the earth offers to us as we place them thankfully at our tables. Are we connected enough with these to be hospitable? Are we willing to offer strangers welcome into those places and relationships and lands we love the most? Are we willing to allow others to call our land their land and our homes their homes? Are we open to immigrants, asylum seekers, refugees, and others? Sometimes it is much easier said than done.

Hospitality makes us fuller, richer, more Christlike people. It's one of the signs that we are a new humanity in Christ. We welcome people into our homes and lives and families and lands in anticipation of the home and the age to come. In doing so we are a foretaste of our ultimate home and of the age to come in Christ Jesus.

One politic. God calls God's church to be a distinct people, with a distinct ethic, a distinct story, a distinct peace, a distinct community, a distinct diversity, and a distinct witness. As Stanley Hauerwas says, "The first responsibility of the church is to *be* the church. . . . The church doesn't *have* a social ethic—the church *is* a social ethic."[12] Put another way, "The church doesn't have a social strategy, the church is a social strategy."[13]

As the new humanity in Jesus Christ, our life together is political. We're not talking here about Republicans or Democrats or some other form of party politics. We're talking about the politics of the realm of God. Together, as God's new creation, we display a new and redeemed politic before a watching world.

Too often we get caught up in the political concerns and spirits of our age. But instead we should show the world a new and redeemed politic by choosing to be the church. What if post-Christendom, secularism, materialism, sexuality, immigrants, refugees, nationalism, and Islam aren't things to be feared but instead opportunities to truly be the church? What if the church could truly be a sanctuary for people needing refuge? In the age of President Trump, certain churches in the United States are becoming sanctuary churches for undocumented workers and their families.[14]

What if these social changes are opportunities to embrace fuller discipleship, to reform our beliefs and practices, to dig deeper into the stories that shape us and our society, to see God's presence within expressions of doubt and questioning, and to practice a distinct social ethic? What if these are opportunities to cultivate a distinct community with a distinct love and ethic and grace and holiness and reconciliation and hope and welcome? What if these are opportunities to discern how we've become thoroughly secularized and how to be the new humanity and new creation in Christ? What if these are opportunities to ask what really shapes our identities and desires and to repent? What if these are opportunities to join with God in God's mission, to live full and joyful lives, to listen to the hopes and longings of others, to embrace fresh confidence in the gospel, to open our hearts and homes and lands and families, and to invite the Spirit to convert its church?

The church remembers, tells, and embodies the story of Jesus Christ. It shows the world what God calls the world to be. The church does not withdraw from the world. The church does not stand in self-righteous judgment on the world.[15] Instead the church serves Jesus and his world. Hauerwas writes, "The church can never abandon the world to the hopelessness deriving from its rejection of God, but must be a people with a hope sufficiently fervid to sustain the world as well as itself."[16] The church, sure of its unique identity, must engage fully with the world—showing the world what God destines it to be.

The church witnesses to Jesus as a peaceable, virtuous, ethical, just, serving, and diverse-but-unified community.[17] God calls the church to be an alternative society. The church is a parallel and distinct community, subverting the present powers and age, providing a standard and vanguard for the world as a foretaste of the age to come.

As a redeemed people, embodying a distinct way of life that witnesses to Jesus and his realm, the church needs to cultivate its unique practices. This way its "body politic," ethic, witness, and social forms are countercultural, missional, and glorifying of Christ. We are called to be "alternative people" or "another city," people who practice a distinct, Christ-honoring life together. The church is salt and light, a "city on a hill."

As part of the church's call to embrace a distinct social existence, we reject violence, relinquish power, pursue holiness, embrace ethics, cultivate meaningful community, embrace missional presence, respect free association, and imitate the servant nature of Christ. A faithful church abandons the reach for power, prestige, and effectiveness that we may often see in megachurches around the world. Rather, it imitates the foolish weakness of the cross. As we look at history, we see God's sovereign purposes unfolding, including the formation of a new, redeemed humanity in Jesus Christ, as reflected in the church's unified politic.

One righteousness. This new people is made holy and righteous by God's grace. God purifies God's people and cleanses them from sin. God sanctifies them so that together they are God's holy and righteous bride. This is all God's work and all according to his grace, a righteousness by faith in Christ alone. We are now "justified freely by his grace through the redemption that came by Christ Jesus. God presented Christ as a sacrifice of atonement, through the shedding of his blood—to be received by faith" (Rom 3:24-25). The Messiah is righteous and makes his people holy, pure, and just through faith in him.

Receiving this righteousness through grace and faith, the new humanity chooses to put aside greed, lust, control, division, prejudice, racism, sexism, and vanity. Together we defy and dismantle unrighteous borders, injustices, divisions, and enmities. Together we clothe ourselves with the new self, which is being renewed in Christ. We embrace unity, humility, self-sacrifice, love, honor, hope, forgiveness, peace, and reconciliation. All these are expressions of our righteousness in Christ (Col 3:1-4:6, 1 Pet 1:13-25).

One peace. God calls the church to be a people of peacemaking and reconciliation. The Messiah is our peace, and he has abolished the conflicts and enmities that divide people (Eph 2:11-14). Peace and reconciliation are at the very heart of the new humanity in Christ. Jesus calls his church to express peace and unity, to be a peaceable community. He calls his church to be peacemakers in a world characterized by misunderstanding, war, hatred, and animosity.

Jesus Christ showed us what peacemaking looks like by living a life of nonviolence, justice, reconciliation, and forgiveness. Not only did he say, "Blessed are the peacemakers, for they will be called children of God" (Mt 5:9), but he also showed us in his life and death what such peacemaking looks like. Love for enemies is the hallmark of discipleship: "Love your enemies and pray for those who persecute you, that you may be children of your Father in heaven" (Mt 5:44-45).

God not only calls us to be peacemakers who love our enemies, but God also "reconciled us to himself through Christ and gave us the ministry of reconciliation" (2 Cor 5:18). God reconciles the world to Godself through Christ. God calls us to be ambassadors of Spirit-empowered reconciliation—calling women and men to be reconciled to God and to each other.

One mission. Taking our cue from David Bosch and Michael Frost, we're convinced that being missional means alerting everyone everywhere to the universal reign of God through Jesus Christ.[18] We do this together, in word, sign, and deed.

The new humanity in Christ integrates proclamation, evangelism, church planting, and social transformation in a seamless whole. We do this best as we learn from each other through multicultural, multiethnic, and global-local conversations. We engage in mission together, locally and globally, alerting people "to the universal reign of God in Christ."[19]

Much of the missional conversation in the West is white, male, and privileged. Such authors have a place, of course, and they have important things to say. But white, male, privileged voices must not dominate our understanding of missional theology and practice. This does the conversation a disservice and doesn't reflect new-humanity church. More than that: it limits, distorts, and even corrupts missional conversations and practices.

We're very hopeful and excited about diverse, multicultural, multiethnic, multivoiced, female-male, global-local missional conversations. These conversations are happening more and more, all over the globe, and it's thrilling. Missional conversations and practices will only be worthwhile if we embrace diversity, multiethnicity, and global voices. We need the perspectives of the Majority World (Third

World), First Nations, indigenous, African American, and diaspora (immigrant) voices. After all, this is where most of the global growth and mission of the church is happening today. A global missional conversation needs voices from all over the planet. It needs the contributions of both genders and of many cultures and ethnicities.

One faith. Our faith is in Jesus the Messiah and his gospel of salvation. This new people—formed as Christ joins Jew and Gentile together as one in him—embraces confident faith in him and his gospel. We say with conviction, "For I am not ashamed of the gospel, because it is the power of God that brings salvation to everyone who believes: first to the Jew, then to the Gentile" (Rom 1:16).

Christians are passionate about many things, which is a good thing. Many issues deserve our passionate and courageous response—politics, race, gender, sexuality, poverty, the environment, and more. But our first passion must be for Jesus and for his gospel—all our other passions must flow out of this first and essential passion.

The gospel is astonishing. The gospel is the story of the triune God working through the story of Israel to save all humanity. The gospel is the story of God bringing that saving work to completion in the saving story of Jesus and in his Lordship over the whole world and all created things. The gospel is the invitation to all people to respond and enter into this marvelous work of God in history in Jesus Christ. This story must capture our hearts, minds, and passions.

In 1 Corinthians 15:3-4, it says that the gospel is "of first importance: that Christ died for our sins according to the Scriptures, . . . he was buried, . . . he was raised on the third day according to the Scriptures." How does this gospel shape our lives, communities, beliefs, and passions? "For Christ's love compels us, because we are convinced that one died for all, and therefore all died. And he died for all, that those who live should no longer live for themselves but for him who died for them and was raised again" (2 Cor 5:14-15).

This gospel is for all people and unites us together in Christ as one. We are united, even in our great diversity, through our shared faith in the power and truth of the gospel. Paul writes, "May the God of hope fill you with all joy and peace as you trust in him, so that you may overflow with hope by the power of the Holy Spirit" (Rom 15:13; see all of Rom 15:7-13 on the inclusivity of the gospel). Our faith unites us as one and fills us with hope.

One hope. Peter exclaims ecstatically,

> Praise be to the God and Father of our Lord Jesus Christ! In his great mercy he has given us new birth into a living hope through the resurrection of Jesus Christ from the dead, and into an inheritance that can never perish, spoil or fade. This inheritance is kept in heaven for you, who through faith are shielded by God's power until the coming of the salvation that is ready to be revealed in the last time. (1 Pet 1:3-5)

The church is experiencing more suffering and persecution today than ever before, all over the globe. And as the world becomes more divided and polarized, it threatens to suck the church into similar conflicts. But we have a living, imperishable, astonishing, and unfading hope! We are aware of our weaknesses and mistakes and failings. But, by the grace and Spirit of God, we are united as a new, restored, and transformed humanity in Christ. This is to result in "praise, glory and honor when Jesus Christ is revealed" (1 Pet 1:7).

We look with hopeful expectation to the end of the age.

> There before me was a great multitude that no one could count, from every nation, tribe, people and language, standing before the throne and before the Lamb. They were wearing white robes and were holding palm branches in their hands. And they cried out in a loud voice:
>
> > "Salvation belongs to our God,
> > who sits on the throne,
> > and to the Lamb." (Rev 7:9-10; see also Rev 5:9-10)

Since our hope is in the age to come, we should seek to be that church now. We must strive to be the unity-in-diversity church, alerting everyone everywhere to the universal reign of God in Christ through our courageous, distinct, countercultural, new-humanity life together.

One love. How will people recognize the new humanity in Christ? They will know we are his people by our love for our enemies and by our love for one another (Mt 5:43-48; Jn 13:34-35).

What does this love look like? Pray for those who persecute you. Forgive those who have wronged you. Seek the welfare of your city and neighborhood, including those who oppose you. Welcome the stranger. Offer refuge, shelter, and hospitality to the undocumented immigrant, the asylum seeker, and the refugee. (This is now becoming more necessary in the United States.) Care for creation. Give away your time, goods, money, and gifts. Stop judging others. Imitate Christ's humility. "Do nothing out of selfish ambition or vain conceit. Rather, in humility value others above yourselves, not looking to your own interests but each of you to the interests of the others. In your relationships with one another, have the same mindset as Christ Jesus" (Phil 2:3-5). Those are just a few of the ways we express love.

We were baptized by the Spirit into one body in Christ, to the glory of God (1 Cor 12:13). As one body with many members, God calls us to prefer each other over ourselves. God calls us to honor and respect our weaker members, to care for each other, to seek unity in our diversity, and to suffer and rejoice together. We use our gifts to serve and build each other up. Finally, we express the gift of love (1 Cor 12:14-31).

We are told what new-humanity love looks like. It is patient, humble, polite, hospitable, warm, forgiving, patient, hopeful, trusting, and persistent. It has no place for sexism, racism, homophobia, classism, greed, pride, prejudice, manipulation, animosity, or fear. "Love never fails" (1 Cor 13:8). "Perfect love drives out fear" (1 Jn 4:18). John puts it succinctly: "God is love. Whoever lives in love lives in God, and God in them" (1 Jn 4:16).

New-humanity churches know that as one body they have one Messiah, one Spirit, one life, one table, one politic, one righteousness, one peace, one mission, one faith, one hope, and one love.

PRACTICES, CHALLENGES, AND ACTIVITIES FOR SMALL GROUPS

Here are some practices and activities for your small group. These will help you reimagine the new humanity in Christ.[20]

Serve with other groups in your community. As a small group, find practical and tangible ways to collaborate with Christians from a variety of backgrounds. Do this in your local community. Serve with Christians from different ethnicities, denominations, theological traditions, ages, approaches to mission and witness, and so on. Now expand this out to collaboration with non-Christian groups that are trying to make a difference in your community. These include social, welfare, religious, governmental groups, and so on. Make sure the collaboration is practical and rooted in your local community. Then get your group to ask questions about their discoveries. What have they learned about mission, partnership, social action, grace, and embrace in these tangible acts of collaboration?

Visit with Christians from a different race and ethnicity from your own. Once every eight weeks, visit a worship service, Bible study, discipleship-training event, prayer meeting, or mission program conducted by Christians from a different ethnicity from your own. Mix it up over a two- or three-year period. This way you've experienced these things in as many ethnic contexts as possible—African American, Arabic, European, Chinese, Greek, Latinx, indigenous Australian, Native American, Pacific Islander, Serbian, South Korean, and so on. Or commit to spending twelve months immersed in a neighborhood and church of an ethnicity other than your own. As a small group, ask questions about what you can learn from these ethnicities and cultures.

Start "listen and learn" nights. During these nights, invite someone from a different faith, ethnicity, theological perspective, and so on to come and share. Invite them to share their story and their views in an attentive, nonthreatening environment. Your aim is not to criticize or debate them. It is to listen and learn. It is to reflect together on your learning as a group and on what it means to be the new humanity in Christ. Your group may never share all the perspectives or theologies of your visitor—especially if they contradict your biblical convictions. But you will grow together as you listen, and especially as you listen with respect, humility, prayer, grace, and attention to the Spirit.

TWO

RENEW LAMENT

In his book *Mirror to the Church*, Emmanuel Katongole reflects on the Rwandan genocide. Katongole says that Rwanda is a "mirror to the church" that compels the church to embrace a new identity in Christ. Before the Rwandan genocide, the majority of Rwandans were Christians. Yet in 1994, beginning on the Easter weekend, "Christians killed other Christians, often in the same churches where they had worshiped together. The most Christianized country in Africa became the site of its worst genocide."[1]

Katongole says that Rwanda is an extreme example of what happens when ethnic, tribal, national, or other identities take the place of our identity in Christ. Rwanda is an extreme example, but it's a mirror to the church. Rwanda mirrors the deep brokenness of the church, the need for repentance, and the hope that is ours in Jesus Christ. A new church has emerged after the Rwandan genocide. It's been slow and difficult, but through grace, forgiveness, and reconciliation this Rwandan church is embracing a new identity in Jesus Christ—not as Hutu or Tutsi but as part of the new humanity in Christ.

Reflecting on the Rwandan genocide, Katongole says, "The resurrection of the church begins with lament."[2] This is difficult for many Americans and others living in Western countries to grasp. Our culture teaches us to embrace a triumphalistic and success-oriented posture. Thus we avoid lament. Americans are prone to move quickly to try to fix things, and often we need to lament, mourn, and grieve first to fully experience and understand what has taken place. In cases of injustice and atrocities such as genocide, the only real response we can have at first is to lament. Scripture teaches us that we can't move toward hope, peace, transformation, and reconciliation without going through sorrow, mourning, regret, and lament.

Prayers of lament are central to Scripture and especially the book of Psalms. More than a third of the psalms are laments. Psalm 142 begins,

> I cry aloud to the LORD;
>> I lift up my voice to the LORD for mercy.
> I pour out before him my complaint;
>> before him I tell my trouble.
> When my spirit grows faint within me,
>> it is you who watch over my way. (Ps 142:1-3)

These psalms of lament focus on deep regret and sorrow for the sins and travails of a nation and as a cry for God's intervention. The people address these laments to God. They describe the lamentable situation, confess their sin and complicity and sorrow, call God to intervene and to change the situation, and offer thanksgiving and praise to God in trust that God can and will bring change. These psalms provide a model for contemporary lament.

The book of Lamentations is five distinct poetic laments for the destruction of Jerusalem. The book follows a similar pattern to the psalms of lament. Lamentations 1 describes the lamentable, sorrowful, and shameful situation. Lamentations 2 connects the pain and suffering with national sins and God's anger at his proud, idolatrous, and sinful people. This is a prayer of confession and lament. Lamentations 3 speaks of the hope for God's mercy and intervention. Lamentations 4 connects ruin and desolation with corporate sins and abuses. Lamentations 5 is a prayer for mercy that God would bring healing, hope, and restoration as the people come to God in repentance. Like the psalms of lament, the book of Lamentations provides a model for present-day lament.

Lament is a demonstrative, strong, and corporate expression of deep grief, pain, sorrow, and regret. Lament and repentance deal with issues of the heart. They pave the way for outer change. Lament is a personal and corporate response to many things: evil, sin, death, harm, discrimination, inequality, racism, sexism, colonization, oppression, and injustice. It is about mourning the painful, shameful, or sorrowful situation, about confessing sin and complicity and sorrow, about calling God to intervene and to change the situation. Finally, lament is about offering thanksgiving and praise to God, knowing that God will intervene and bring change, hope, and restoration.

WHY DO WE NEED TO LAMENT?

Lament is about regretting and mourning the past and then moving toward repentance, justice, and new life together. Patricia Huntington states, "We suffer and labor in travail, this is the stuff of lamentation."[3] From there we move toward hope.

Lament is necessary for repentance, healing, wholeness, and hope. It challenges injustice, racism, exploitation, and the status quo. Walter Brueggemann says that when "lament as a form of speech and faith is lost" (as it currently is in North America), the church loses its ability to confront and redress abuses, wrongs, and inequalities. "A theological monopoly is reinforced, docility and submissiveness are engendered, and the outcome in terms of social practice is to reinforce and consolidate the political-economic monopoly of the status quo."[4]

Soong-Chan Rah writes, "The American church avoids lament. The power of lament is minimized and the underlying narrative of suffering that requires lament is lost. . . . The absence of lament in the liturgy of the American church results in the loss of memory. We forget the necessity of lamenting over suffering and pain. We forget the reality of suffering and pain."[5] The United States suffers from amnesia. It is time that the United States recovers its memory and laments for our sins.

Lament becomes a crucial practice as we embrace the new humanity in Jesus Christ. We must enter lament and repentance to experience reconciliation, justice, unity, peace, and love.

WHAT DO WE LAMENT?

We lament the exploitation and destruction of black lives and communities; the abuse of basic human rights; and systemic injustice, expressed in policing, judicial, educational, economic, social, and other systems and structures. We lament the murders of Alton B. Sterling, Philando Castile, the five Dallas police officers, and the numerous black women and men killed in this and previous centuries. We lament the United States' demons, as Willie James Jennings writes:

> Is America willing to be freed from its demons? . . . Racial antagonism structures our imaginations as does our love of weapons. The former creates our enemies, and the latter constructs a false sense of independence and freedom. . . . We have learned to structure our fear geographically and unleash it through police violence set up to protect our spaces. Land developers, civil engineers, city planners, real estate agencies, builders, insurance companies and a whole host of others all profit from our barrier-building and fear-mongering. . . . We have been in a racial cold war for centuries, and now a real war beckons us. . . . The demons tempt us to violence, but there has always been a way to resist that temptation. We must follow the way of a God who will not release us either to our demons or to our despair.[6]

We lament corruption among politicians, police forces, and bankers; military interventions and the militarization of society and police forces; uncaring government agencies and big business; and urban poverty and homelessness. We lament the enslavement, rape, exploitation, and oppression of people of color and their communities; systems of slavery and institutionalized racism; the proliferation of guns in society, and the idolatry and death associated with gun cultures; the violation and oppression of women (and especially black women); and the way people and people groups have been imprisoned instead of rehabilitated. We lament rampant Islamophobia, reinforced by Donald Trump's announcement of a ban of people from seven Muslim-dominated countries from entering the United States. We lament the nature, extent, and effects of white privilege, nationalism, xenophobia, and racism; the unwelcome shown to refugees and asylum seekers; and the fear, anxiety, and suffering experienced by undocumented migrants.

We lament the treatment of women in society and church. Too often women suffer multiple oppressions. We lament gender inequalities, the discrimination and harassment women suffer, the sexualization of women and girls, and the domestic violence many women suffer daily. We lament the sex trafficking of poor young Asian girls whose bodies are sold for sex, domination, and exploitation. We lament the theological and religious constructs that seek to make women subordinate, submissive, and silent.

We lament the colonization, devastation, and assimilation of First Nations and indigenous peoples, and the role Christianity has played in this. We lament colonialism, paternalism, expansionism, and the oppressive dimensions of Christendom. We lament the United States' segregated churches and neighborhoods, its near-genocide of Native American peoples, and its enslavement of one another. We lament the United States' original sins: racism, sexism, and addiction to power.[7] We lament American exceptionalism and all its effects, predatory lenders and real estate speculators, and the colonization and devastation of Native American and indigenous and aboriginal cultures.

We lament America's treatment of Latinx immigrants and the pain and trauma caused to those who are undocumented. While Christian faith is vibrant among Latinx immigrants, many feel unwelcome, marginalized, and discriminated against. We lament the treatment of Asian immigrants who worked as indentured workers and who died building the railroad. Those who survived never made enough money to go back home.

In Australia we lament our treatment of Aboriginal and Torres Strait Islander peoples, the high level of violence against women, the spread of Islamophobia, and our treatment of asylum seekers on the high seas and in offshore detention centers.

We lament when my Muslim friend is called racial slurs and when my Asian American friend is told to "go back to China." We lament when my Asian American dad is called "chink" and "worthless Chinaman" because racism exists and is breeding hate.

We lament the silence of the people of God about many of these things. We lament the complicity of the church in many of these things.

This practice of lament is necessary if we are to experience healing and hope and transformation.

HOW DO WE LAMENT?

The personal nature of lament is important. But lament is best when it's both individual and corporate.

The psalms of lament and the book of Lamentations provide a model for present-day lament. This model is flexible and adaptable and shouldn't be used rigidly. But it shows us that lament typically has nine elements:

1. *Invocation.* We address our lament to God. "How long, LORD?" (Ps 13:1).

2. *Worship.* We describe who God is (loving, just, merciful, and good) and how God promises to be with us in times of crisis.

"Yet you are enthroned as the Holy One; you are the one Israel praises" (Ps 22:3).

3. *Description.* We describe the lamentable, sorrowful, and shameful situation. Complaint about the problem and description of the problem often go together in lament. This is often expressed as questions to God (a) about God's action or inaction, (b) about our enemies, (c) and/or about our suffering and pain. "Dogs surround me" (Ps 22:16).

4. *Connection.* We connect the lamentable situation and our pain and suffering with individual and corporate sins (such as pride, racism, sexism, idolatry, power seeking, fear-mongering, etc.). "We are consumed by your anger and terrified by your indignation. You have set our iniquities before you, our secret sins in the light of your presence" (Ps 90:7-8).

5. *Repentance.* We express deep sorrow for the sins and travails of our people, and our desire to change. "If only we knew the power of your anger! Your wrath is as great as the fear that is your due. Teach us to number our days, that we may gain a heart of wisdom" (Ps 90:11-12).

6. *Confession.* We confess our sin, complicity, sorrow, and desire to repent and change. "We have sinned, even as our ancestors did; we have done wrong and acted wickedly" (Ps 106:6).

7. *Petition.* We cry for God's intervention and mercy, and that God would bring healing, hope, and restoration as we come to God in lament and repentance. "Relent, LORD! How long will it be? Have compassion on your servants. Satisfy us in the morning with your unfailing love, that we may sing for joy and be glad all our days" (Ps 90:13-14).

8. *Trust.* We express our trust in God because of who God is and in remembrance of God's past saving and redeeming actions.

We acknowledge that God listens and responds, "From the horns of the wild oxen you have rescued me" (Ps 22:21 NRSV).

9. *Praise.* We offer thanksgiving and praise to God for who God is and what God has done. We offer praise in trust that God can and will bring change. "From you comes the theme of my praise in the great assembly" (Ps 22:25).

In chapters two and three of *Prophetic Lament*, Soong-Chan Rah makes two important observations about lament. First, the genre of lament is *funeral dirge.* Second, lament provides opportunities for us to hear and respond to the voices of the silenced, marginalized, and suffering. After the murders of Alton B. Sterling, Philando Castile, and five Dallas police officers, Soong-Chan Rah summarized these two observations in this way:

(1) Lamentations deals with a funeral, not a hospital visit (See Lam 1, 2, 4). We cannot pretend that the problem of racism is solved by a hospital visit: a quick prayer and the person will leave the hospital eventually. Our racial history is littered with abused, beaten, murdered dead bodies of black men and women. If you do not acknowledge the long history of dead bodies, you are only playing the game of reconciliation. (2) Lamentations offers the opportunity to hear from all the voices that have suffered. While a prophet/narrator (probably Jeremiah) compiles the laments, it is really the voice of the suffering: women, children, orphans, widows, the sick, the lame and the blind. IT IS NOT the voice of the privileged that is lifted up. Listen and relay the voices of the suffering today. Do not spin the events of this past week to make your own culturally-based application of "personal responsibility" or "law and order." Lamentations speaks the voice of the suffering not the voice of the privileged.[8]

The practice of lament is crucial for the healing, reconciliation, and transformation of the church.

WHAT DO LAMENTS LOOK LIKE?

Following the nine elements of lament listed above, we recommend you practice writing your own lament. Here are two examples of laments. Both are adapted from Lamentations 5.

Grace wrote the first one as a lament for Sandra Bland, who was found hanged in a jail cell in Texas on July 13, 2015. This was three days after being arrested during a traffic stop. Her death was ruled as a suicide and was followed by public protests that disputed the cause of death and instead alleged racial violence. Graham wrote the second lament for Australia's treatment of Aboriginal and Torres Strait Islander peoples.

You may design different kinds of laments, but we hope these can serve as examples to get you started.

A lament for Sandra Bland.

1 God who creates and loves us all,
> We turn to you as we lament the death of Sandra Bland.

2 You are a creative God,
> You made Sandra and each of us in your image.

3 Yet society failed to welcome Sandra, rejecting her and her beautiful, young, black body.
> She died hanging in a jail cell.

4 Her unexplained death rips an unspeakable hole in her family as they lose a daughter and a sister.
> Her friends experience a profound loss. Grief remains.

5 You are a comforting God. You understand the sorrows, grief, and agony of your children.
> You stand with Sandra's family and friends in their grief.

6 Inspire us to stand with those who love Sandra,
> and demand justice for her death.

7 You are a loving God. You create a diverse humanity to love
you and to love one another.

Our value comes from you as our Creator.

8 We confess we fall short of your intentions.

We judge and discriminate against one other; we wound
and violate each other.

9 We have created and sustained a system based on the sin
of racism,

which proclaims that the color of our skin gives us value.

10 Racism denies your love for all your children;

denies your invitation to us to love one another.

11 Racism privileges some of your children and oppresses others,

giving rise to events such as the death of Sandra Bland.

12 You are a merciful God. Forgive us for how we fall short.

Pour your Holy Spirit afresh upon us. Open us to the
healing you offer. Draw us together.

13 Lead us from despair to wholeness,

that we might love one another and work to end racism.

14 You are a faithful God.

We give thanks for the life and love and witness of
Sandra Bland.

15 We give thanks for the ways you are at work within the
brokenness of our lives,

and the woundedness of our communities and nation.

16 We give thanks that through Jesus we are freed to join in
your work;

through the Holy Spirit we are empowered to join in your
transformational work.

17 Through Jesus we pray,

Amen.

A lament for Australia.

1 Remember, O Lord, what has happened to us;
> look, and see our disgrace.

2 Our nation has ignored and denied the inheritance of
ancient cultures,
> the desert, fresh water, and sea peoples,
> who've lived here for 60,000 years.

3 Over 500 Aboriginal and Torres Strait Islander nations have
been displaced,
> lands and children have been stolen.

4 We ask for recognition and basic human rights,
> dignity and freedom for all Australians alike.

5 Those who pursue us are at our heels;
> we are weary and find no rest.

6 We submitted to those who introduced new diseases,
forcibly acquired lands,
> and thrived on violent conflict and colonization.

7 Our ancestors invaded this beautiful land and are no more,
> but we, Aboriginal and Torres Strait Islander and
> non-Indigenous peoples together,
> bear the shame and enmity and suffering.

8 Slavery, colonization, and invasion oppressed us,
> and we cried out for freedom from their hands.

9 We get our bread at the risk of our lives,
> young and old are imprisoned and forgotten.

10 Our skin is hot as an oven,
> chained, beaten, imprisoned, and murdered, in the
> blazing outback sun.

11 Colonizers have violated women since Australia's earliest days,
> and we mourn Stolen Generations.

12 Children and adults have been hung by their hands,
   murdered and driven off cliffs,
      elders are shown no respect.

13 Children and youth are in our jails, separated from culture
   and family,
      mothers are in refuges or on the streets.

14 The elders still speak, but our nation does not listen,
      the Dreamtime continues to show our nation another way.

15 Joy is gone from our hearts;
      our dancing has turned to mourning and lament.

16 The crown of colonization and cultural superiority has
   fallen from our head.
      Woe to us, for we have sinned!

17 Because of this our hearts are faint,
      because of these things our eyes grow dim,

18 for Aboriginal and Torres Strait Islander people,
      with loan sharks, drug dealers, corrupt officials, and
      others, prowling about us.

19 You, O Lord, reign forever;
      you live among Aboriginal and Torres Strait Islander nations,
         and among non-Indigenous Australians,
            on this beautiful and sacred and ancient land,
               since time immemorial.

20 We witness the vibrancy of Aboriginal and Torres Strait
   Islander cultures,
      your presence in art, music, languages, beliefs,
      and practices.

21 Restore us to yourself, Lord, that we may return;
      renew our days as of old,

22 unless you have utterly rejected us,
   and are angry with us beyond measure.

23 Restore to us a heart of flesh,
   rid us of our heart of stone.

24 Restore in us a desire for justice and truth,
   a desire to see all people restored to their place and lands.

25 Speak to us through your Spirit,
   present in the voices and cultures and desires of ancient
   and modern peoples.

26 Rid us of one-sided or superficial calls for reconciliation,
   and lead us toward true lament and repentance and justice.

PRACTICES, CHALLENGES, AND ACTIVITIES FOR SMALL GROUPS

Here are some practices and activities for your small group. These will
help you explore and experience lament.

Write a group lament. Following the nine elements of lament,
spend some time in your small group writing and sharing your laments. Remember, you don't need to be rigid or legalistic with the
elements. Be flexible, adaptable, and creative as you write a lament.
Make the lament your own. What breaks your heart? What weighs
you down? What grieves you in church and culture? What relationships or situations bring you pain? What do you rage against? What
do you mourn? What do you feel regret for? What do you confess?
Write a lament together as a small group, following these steps.

1. Together choose an issue or subject that angers or grieves your
   group. It might be racial injustice, environmental destruction, the
   treatment of undocumented immigrants, or some other issue.

2. Brainstorm why this issue is important and why it angers,
   grieves, and pains your group.

3. Write a lament together, structured around these nine stages or elements (described earlier): invocation, worship, description, connection, lament, confession, petition, trust, and praise. You might do this by asking people in pairs to write one or two of these nine stages or elements.

4. Ask one or two people to read your finished lament aloud so you can get a sense of how it sounds as spoken word.

5. Spend time together in prayer over the themes in the lament.

6. At the end of the time of prayer, have someone read your group's lament aloud once again.

7. During the week, make sure everyone in your group gets a copy of your shared lament. You may even ask your pastor whether you can share your group lament during a Sunday service.

Organize a lament table liturgy (an evening of shared lament in your small group). The Practice is a group that meets regularly for experimental worship in South Barrington, Illinois. On their website they provide a model for a small group evening of lament.[9] They call it a "Lament Table Liturgy." Here's a summary of that model:

1. Send out invites to a small group of Christians, asking them to join you for a night of shared lament. Choose people you want to connect with, and choose people who are different from you (if possible, try to make your group a mix of genders, ages, ethnicities, etc.). In the invite, explain what lament is and why it is important.

2. Ask those who are coming to the evening of lament to write their own lament. Encourage them to follow the guide provided by The Practice.[10] This guide gives people nine steps for writing their own lament.

3. At the beginning of the evening, share a meal together around a common table. Hospitality, welcome, friendship, and food provide the perfect environment for shared lament.

4. Create holy space by praying the liturgy of lament. This is a "table liturgy" because it is shared around a common table. Use the beautiful table liturgy created by Kellye Fabian and The Practice community.[11] Make sure you print off a copy of the table liturgy for each person attending the evening of lament. Provide them with a candle too. This candle is a symbol of the lamentable situation, of their cry to God, and of their hope.

5. Enjoy the "Lament Table Liturgy" together. Commit to finding fresh and creative ways to engage in praise and lament.

THREE

REPENT TOGETHER

O ur world is plagued by the pursuit of power and control, and by injustices, exploitations, and racial disparities. These are political, social, and racial problems. But they are also personal and social sins.

Sins such as racism affect both our society and our personal lives. Racial disparity in the United States criminal justice system is an example. According to the Sentencing Project, "African-American males are six times more likely to be incarcerated than white males and 2.5 times more likely than Latino males. If current trends continue, one of every three black American males born today can expect to go to prison in his lifetime, as can one of every six Latino males—compared to one of every seventeen white males."[1] The sin of racism has had a devastating impact on African Americans and had led to both explicit racial discrimination and in effect the construction of two distinct criminal justice systems ("one for wealthy people and another for poor people and minorities").[2]

As God's people, we must embrace repentance and change. These are the right responses to racism, sexism, greed, and other forms of social and personal sin. But what is repentance?

Repentance involves key changes in people, groups, and communities. It includes our minds, hearts, and wills. Repentance can be personal, but it can also be corporate. Repentance includes a *metanoia*, a change of mind and a turning around. Scripture says, "Repent, then, and turn to God, so that your sins may be wiped out, that times of refreshing may come from the Lord" (Acts 3:19). Acts 20:21 further says, "I have declared to both Jews and Greeks that they must turn to God in repentance and have faith in our Lord Jesus." Repentance means that we change our ways and turn toward God.

There are individual sins and corporate/community sins. As individuals we sin by ourselves and come to God for forgiveness. We are very aware of our individual sins, as we commit them personally. Corporate sins are committed by society and institutions that we as individuals become complicit in. We fail to speak up against institutional sins such as racism, sexism, and injustice in the criminal justice system. We therefore need to repent of our social sins as well.

Repentance is a four-stage process. The first stage is *conviction*. We recognize that one or more of our attitudes and behaviors are wrong. They are broken and sinful, and they can damage us and others. This conviction of sin grips our hearts and minds. The second stage is *contrition*. We lament, regret, and mourn our mistakes and sins. We feel sorrow and remorse for these attitudes and behaviors, for their effect on people and on the earth, and for their offensiveness to God. Contrition is a godly sorrow that moves us to action.

The third stage is *commitment*. We decide to turn away from our sin and commit to new, God-honoring, and redemptive attitudes, postures, and behaviors. This is changing our minds, changing our attitudes, changing our purpose, changing our desires, and changing our ways. The fourth stage is *change*. We practice a new way of being in the world. This is the way of repentance, righteousness, humility, justice, love, and reconciliation. Godly sorrow leads to faith, hope, and love.

WHY DO WE NEED TO REPENT?

We live in a broken world. This brokenness not only hurts us, it also hurts those around us. We chase after things that we shouldn't that, even when we reach them, leave us feeling unfulfilled. We treat people (including those who love us) in ways that we're ashamed of. We desire and long for the wrong things.

There's a lot of joy and happiness in the world among friends and neighbors. But there's also a lot of brokenness among us—in our relationships, families, businesses, politics, churches, and institutions. Sometimes this brokenness comes through no fault of our own. At other times it's a direct consequence of choices we've made, values we've embraced, and behaviors we've adopted. We must repent of these things before healing and reconciliation can occur. We are all broken in our own way; we've all sinned and made mistakes. But the good news is that there's hope for a new and full life through the path of repentance and change.

We were created to glorify and worship the one holy and eternal God as well as to enjoy intimate relationship with God, creation, and people. Yet this desire for worship and intimacy is often perverted. When we don't worship Jesus Christ, we direct our adoration and gaze toward a host of other things. This leads to brokenness and requires repentance.

We worship control and power.

We worship change and mobility.

We worship privacy and overexposure.

We worship money and prosperity.

We worship accomplishments and status.

We worship competition and free enterprise.

We worship individuality and autonomous expression.

We worship positivity and happiness.

We worship utility and practicality.

We worship sexuality and beauty.

We worship our children and our legacy.

We worship nationalism and patriotism.

We worship freedom and choice.

We worship safety and borders.

We worship image and brand and new media.

We worship experience and distraction.

Yet all this is misdirected and broken worship. It never satisfies. It hurts us, it damages the ones we love, and it wounds all those who come across our path.

We were created for intimacy and for the holiness that arises out of intimacy with a holy God. We as Christians are called by God to discipleship to Jesus Christ as an expression and revelation of divine-human intimacy and holiness. When we don't connect deeply with God (and with creation and people), we direct our desires and passions in self-destructive and other-destructive ways. Our lack of intimacy with a holy God leads to broken relationships and shattered integrity.

Let's take racism and sexism as examples. Many pastors fail to challenge their congregations about this, but racism and sexism are sins. They aren't merely political and social problems—they are rooted in sin.

Yet, the good news is that there is an answer to this sin, and to this broken worship and intimacy. The answer is in repentance and change. Renewed hearts, minds, and behaviors lead to restored relationship with God, with people, and with the earth.

WHAT DO WE REPENT OF?

We've described what repentance is, and we've considered why we need to repent. Now let's explore what we need to repent of. We can't move toward healing and reconciliation without embracing repentance for these things.

Worshiping modern idols. Instead of worshiping and following the Messiah, we often worship modern idols. These contemporary idols never satisfy, and they easily become obsessions. The church is as guilty of this as any other group of people. These modern gods include political power, patriotic hope, cultural status, national leaders, secular philosophies, celebrities, financial wealth, change and mobility, expressive autonomy, progressive or conservative ideologies, and more.

All these gods will disappoint or corrupt us. They are cold, hard stone, unresponsive to our human predicament and unable to offer us healing, salvation, and hope. They are all idols—lesser gods that turn our eyes away from the Son of God.

It's time to repent of this idolatry and return to the worship of Jesus Christ. Only he can offer salvation, healing, reconciliation, peace, and hope.

Pursuing power and control. As we noted above, some say that racism is America's original sin. That may be so, or it may be that racism is an expression of an even deeper sin: the desire for power and control.

There's something seductive about power and control. Our culture would have us believe that we can control people, wealth, politics, nature, and the future. We seek to control time and destiny, story and meaning, history and education, money and privilege, politics and decision making, creation and productivity, peoples and hope. We seek to exercise power and control through goal setting, rhetoric, busyness, the military, monetary policy, religion, sexism, education, politics, legal instruments, and racial discrimination.

So what can we do? We must repent of this passion and desire for power, surrender control, return to dependence on God, and find fresh ways to honor the weak, the foolish, the dishonorable and the powerless. We must determine to relinquish power, embrace what it means to be "the scum of the earth" (1 Cor 4:13), whose approach to life seems foolish yet tells of another way. "But God chose the foolish things of the world to shame the wise; God chose the weak things of the world to shame the strong. God chose the lowly things of the world and the despised things—and the things that are not—to nullify the things that are" (1 Cor 1:27-28).

Confusing religious patriotism with Christian discipleship. Many of us are patriotic. We love our country and want it to prosper. But we should never put love of country over our love for God and our desire for the well-being of our neighbor. We should never confuse love of country with love of God. Religious patriotism can easily tip over into aggressive religious nationalism. Religious patriotism conflates and confuses passion for nation with love for God. Walter Brueggemann writes, "The crisis in the U.S. church has almost nothing to do with being liberal or conservative; it has everything to do with giving up on the faith and discipline of our Christian baptism and settling for a common, generic U.S. identity that is part patriotism, part consumerism, part violence, and part affluence."[3]

Ancient Christians defied allegiance to Rome and to Caesar when they declared, "Jesus is Lord!" They saw themselves as citizens of a different kin-dom, an alternative people, a new nation.[4] Nations and states no longer defined them, nor commanded their love and allegiance. They had transferred this loyalty to Jesus and his kin-dom and church.

Religious patriotism—when it confuses being American (or Australian, or some other nationality) with being a disciple of Jesus—is a darkness that God calls us to repent of. Peter writes, "You are a chosen people, a royal priesthood, a holy nation, God's special possession, that you may declare the praises of him who called you out of darkness into his wonderful light" (1 Pet 2:9).

Believing American exceptionalism. It's time to challenge the sins of exceptionalism. This includes the specific sins of American exceptionalism (the idea that the United States is exceptional and has a divine mandate to lead and dominate global politics, economics, culture, and military force).

Historically many nations have claimed such exceptionalism. These include China, France, Germany, Hellas, India, imperial Japan, Israel, ancient Rome, the Ottoman Empire, North Korea, Spain, Britain, the United States, the USSR, and Thailand. Exceptionalism often integrates with religion. In the American context, this has manifested itself as close ties between American exceptionalism and American civil religion.

But all national exceptionalism is wrong and idolatrous—including American exceptionalism. Exceptionalism is a false god that demands recognition, support, and allegiance.

It is time to repent of American exceptionalism and civil religion. Instead we should embrace what it means to truly be the church, made up of all peoples, tribes, languages, ethnicities, and nations. This church's allegiance is to Jesus Christ, not to any one nation. The church is exceptional because—as a people made up of all peoples and nations—it shows the world what God wants the world to be.

Sanctioning violence. Whenever we sanction violence, we contradict God's peaceable, loving, reconciling, and compassionate kindom. Violence includes sexual violence, racial violence, spiritual violence, psychological violence, emotional violence, physical violence, and more.

Let's take American gun deaths as an example. The United States needs to examine its obsession with guns. When it comes to gun death rates, according to the *New York Times* "the U.S. is in a different world."[5] There were 8,454 gunshot homicides in the United States in 2013. Compare that with 131 in Canada and forty-seven in Australia that same year. Americans love their guns for many reasons, but there is a clear link between this gun culture and gun violence. Failing to address this issue is a form of sanctioning violence.

Violence is committed not only at home but also worldwide by the United States. According to recent figures, the United States dropped about three bombs every hour, twenty-four hours a day. That is a total of 26,171 bombs in 2016.[6] This was by a president who received the Nobel Peace prize in 2009.

Torture is another example of sanctioned violence. Tim Keel writes, "Torture is incompatible with the gospel of Jesus Christ. It is impossible to reconcile faith in Christ with faith in the state using its power this way. That this statement will provoke an angry response from many Christians who support the state using torture is illustrative in itself and a sign of how deeply our faith has been compromised and domesticated."[7]

We repent and ask for God's forgiveness for all the times we've sanctioned violence.

Chasing money and status. The pursuit of wealth and status isn't just a Western problem, but it is certainly entrenched in Western societies. We chase after wealth, fame, and honor, then misuse Scripture to justify our lifestyles and greed.

Jesus had a lot to say about money and status. Jesus challenges us not to store up treasures on earth. Instead we are to seek first the kindom of God and sell our possessions and give to the poor. When we put our time and passion and resources into accumulating wealth and possessions, we show what we really desire and value. We make it clear what we love. "For where your treasure is, there your heart will be also" (Lk 12:34; see Lk 12:13-34; Mt 6:19-24).

Being wealthy and honored and famous isn't the problem—the love and pursuit of these things is the issue. We make these things our idols, and they enslave us. "No one can serve two masters. Either you will hate the one and love the other, or you will be devoted to the one and despise the other. You cannot serve both God and money" (Mt 6:24). You cannot serve both God and ambition, or God and greed, or God and pride.

Instead we should stop concentrating on ourselves, imitate Christ's humility, receive Jesus through humility, be willing to be the poorest and the last. Our confidence is not in our performance or possessions or status but in Christ (Mt 5:3-5; 11:29; 18:3-4; Lk 14:11; 18:14; Rom 3:22-24; Phil 2:8-9; 1 Pet 5:5).

Embracing individualism. Western cultures value rugged individualism and fierce independence. We trade value for value. We applaud those who through individual determination and strength succeed in the face of obstacles and adversities. This worldview says that we are all alone from cradle to grave and need to work hard as autonomous beings to succeed and make our mark. In the meantime, those who cannot succeed are ignored, shunned, and devalued. These include the poor, uneducated, marginalized, ill, elderly, disabled, unemployed, and so on.

But this isn't the way of the kin-dom of God. In God's economy we are part of a community from cradle to grave. We exist and flourish in relationship. The Bible notes that community is important to God. "And let us consider how we may spur one another on toward love and good deeds, not giving up meeting together, as some are in the habit of doing, but encouraging one another—and all the more as you see the Day approaching" (Heb 10:24-25). "How good and pleasant it is when God's people live together in unity!" (Ps 133:1). The redeemed community—the new humanity in Christ—values the weak and the strong, the poor and the rich, and the white person and the person of color. We are a community that embraces and supports those who are struggling, marginalized, unemployed, and impoverished. We love them as Christ loves the church. We value them as much as we value any other member of society or the church.

This new humanity in Christ believes in community, interdependence, compassion, and love.

Fostering disunity and division. The nonpartisan Pew Research Center released research in February 2017 that showed the deep divisions in American society. These divisions run along racial, age, political, and religious lines. They lead to misunderstandings and hostility. Passions run red hot over political and social and racial issues. People feel strongly about President Trump and his policies, and the nation is deeply polarized.

The Pew report looked at views on President Trump's executive order to stop refugees from entering the United States for 120 days and to stop people from seven majority-Muslim countries from entering the United States on a visa for ninety days. White Americans are divided over the policies (49 percent approve, 50 percent disapprove), while most African Americans (84 percent) and Latinx (79 percent) reject these policies. White evangelicals tend to support the policies (76 percent), compared with only 38 percent of the broader American public. Most Catholics (62 percent) and those unaffiliated with religion (74 percent) reject the President's policies. Seventy-six percent of Americans ages eighteen to twenty-nine reject these policies, while older Americans are divided on the issue. Of those who say they are Republican leaning, 81 percent approve of these policies, while Democrat-leaning voters overwhelmingly reject the policies (89 percent).[8]

For those who've been watching traditional and social media, it's clear that these divisions run deep and arouse passion. As an Australian I (Graham) see similar things within Australian society.

What's concerning is the way this division has affected the Christian church. Instead of discussing the policies calmly, empathetically, and respectfully, many Christians have resorted to name calling, accusations, anger, and division. Not only are the divisions in society replicated in the church, but the animosity toward the other is also reflected.

Our world is plagued by deep divisions—racial, political, social, and other. If your Facebook feed is anything like ours, you see people express such misunderstandings and animosities every day. Sadly, the church too often mirrors and repeats these divisions. But Jesus calls the church to replace division and animosity with renewed life

together and in the world—a life of love, peace, reconciliation, forgiveness, thanksgiving, and prayer.

It is time to repent of disunity and division. The church must replace
division with unity, exclusion with embrace, accusations with thanksgiving, animosity with love, fear with hope, and enmity with prayer.

Cultivating racism and sexism. A racialized/racist and gendered/
sexist worldview has infused the Western and Christian social imagination. This worldview shapes the way people, including Christians,
see and live in the world. It gives birth to notions of whiteness and
blackness and of maleness and femaleness.[9] The result is that Christianity has become white and male (even though most members of
the global church are female people of color). Where Christianity
thrives outside male whiteness, this thriving is seen as an abnor-
mality or novelty. It is seen as a weaker, lesser, or suspicious version
of Christianity or theology—an aberration to be ignored, quarantined,
or dismissed. It's either made invisible, or it's made exotic.[10]

We need to repent of this racism and sexism. We need a radical
reorientation of Christianity in the twenty-first century, which fully
embraces all races and sexes. Ignoring or minimizing sexism and racism
is sexism and racism. Ignoring or minimizing sexism and racism in
church and society only gives license for sexism and racism to spread
and grow.

Christians don't have the option of minimizing or ignoring racism
and sexism. We have a responsibility to question and condemn all
sexist or racist attitudes, theologies, practices, and remarks. We have
a responsibility to challenge, confront, and condemn sexism and
racism in all their forms.

Yassir Morsi reminds us that we shouldn't focus only on the
symptoms of racism, such as prejudice, intolerance, and bigotry.
These are symptoms, not racism itself. Morsi says that racism is more
about power than psychology, more about system than sentiment,
and more about denial of agency than denial of acceptance. Sexism

is the same. Both racism and sexism are about the abuse and use of power. They are about systemic injustices, exclusions, and evils, manifest in law, politics, education, business, religion, and more. Morsi says that we don't address such things by trying to make people more "accepting." We need to confront and change the roots of racism (and sexism) by addressing issues of power, systems, and denial of agency.[11]

When we look at how the Western world treats, for example, Native American women, we can see how both racism and sexism come into play. Andrea Smith reminds us that we need to deconstruct Western epistemologies and work toward reconstruction so that we can get rid of the racism and sexism embedded within Christianity. She challenges the natural and historical understanding of Christianity and notes how indigenous peoples see Christianity not as liberative but rather as domineering. The dominant white society is superior, and the Native communities are "savage."[12]

What kind of racist and sexist attitudes does the church need to repent of? Here are some examples: Women are objects to be sexualized and exploited. Only attractive women have any value. Men can exploit their power for their sexual gratification and the sake of their ego needs. Women are manipulative and can't be trusted. Other ethnicities (especially "nonwhites") are inferior. It's normal to fear and distrust the strange racial or sexual other. The pain of white people is more important than the pain of minorities, undocumented immigrants, and people of color. Other races are corrupting our society, taking our jobs, and ruining our faith and identity. Everything will be okay if people like us (especially white men) get back in power again. *All the attitudes in this paragraph are vile.*

So what can we do?

We can be outraged. And we can examine the ways we have harbored sexism and racism in our own lives and families and churches. And we can repent and change and rip these things out by the roots.

We can refuse to ignore, minimize, or disregard sexist or racist views and remarks. We can speak up in rallies or write posts to bring awareness to the sexism and racism that persist daily. I (Grace) have attended rallies such as Black Lives Matter to actively repent for the sins of racism. I have also signed petitions and was a signatory for the "Theological Declaration on Christian Faith and White Supremacy." It is a national appeal to Christian congregations against white supremacy, terrorism, and nationalism.[13]

We can demand an apology from those who express such opinions. We can demand a commitment to relinquish these views and never make such remarks again.

We can speak up whenever public figures make derogatory statements about women, minorities, and immigrants.

We can question and condemn all sexist or racist attitudes and remarks (no matter who they come from—colleague, classmate, teacher, friend, family member, president, or president-elect).

We can stop organizing and speaking at all–white male conferences and panels.[14]

We can recognize that women are the heartbeat of living faith.[15]

We can recognize the church's complicity in oppressing, dispossessing, and silencing indigenous peoples (Native Americans, First Nations peoples, Aboriginal and Torres Straight Islanders, Māori peoples, etc.). We can allow the gospel to be "rescued from the cowboys."[16]

We can show another way: respecting and valuing women, and treating other ethnicities and cultures with the dignity they deserve.

We can strive to live blameless lives (both individually and in Christian community) that glorify and witness to Jesus Christ and that stand in contrast to the destructive, demeaning, derogatory, and divisive spirits of this age.

We can repent, change, and follow the way of Christ.

Closing our hearts to refugees and migrants. There is a powerful scene in *The Fellowship of the Ring* where the elf-lord Gildor Inglorion reminds Frodo and his friends that the Shire is part of a wider world that they have responsibility for. "It is not your own Shire," says Gildor. "Others dwelt here before hobbits were; and others will dwell here again when hobbits are no more. The wide world is all about you: you can fence yourselves in, but you cannot forever fence it out."[17]

The UNHCR's "Global Trends 2012 Report—Displacement: The New 21st Century Challenge" analyzes trends among refugees, asylum seekers, returnees, stateless persons, and groups of internally displaced persons (IDPs). The report estimates that in 2012 almost fifty million people were forcibly displaced worldwide. Persecution, conflict, violence, and human-rights violations caused these people to flee their homes. Developing countries hosted over 80 percent of the world's refugees. Children (those below eighteen years old) made up 50 percent of the refugee population.[18]

In the United States President Trump ran on the platform that he will build a big wall between the United States and Mexico. He is hard on immigration and is actively deporting undocumented people back to their countries. As a result families are being separated, and children are losing their parents. The effects will be long lasting.

Graham's daughter Madison April Hill reviewed M. Daniel Carroll R.'s *Christians at the Border* for the GlobalChurch Project in 2016.[19] She writes,

> The immigration debate is important in our modern world. We see this in North America, the Asia-Pacific, Europe, and other continents. The debate is especially vigorous in my country, Australia, where issues to do with immigration, asylum seekers, and refugees are discussed passionately. Carroll's book is essential to the current debate as it provides a strong viewpoint that helps to represent Christian faith on this topic. [Carroll says that] *"Christians at the Border* above all else strives to motivate believers of the majority culture and Latinos to begin thinking, talking, and acting as Christians in regard to immigration."[20]

We Christians have closed our hearts and homes and lands to refugees, asylum seekers, migrants, and undocumented immigrants for too long. This has led to immeasurable suffering among the world's most vulnerable people. How should Christians respond to such need? Through repentance, welcome, and hospitality, we can begin to make changes in our world.

I (Grace) have taken a couple of classes to the United States–Mexico border through an organization called Borderlinks. This program allows students and churches to experience some of the hardships that migrants face for their desire to come into the United States. Through this educational program, many people change their minds and attitudes about migrant workers. They come to realize that they are not all criminals, and all they want to have is a better life for their families. Along the border there are several safe places that migrants can go to for safety and rest that my classes have visited. Once you meet the migrants and enjoy a meal together, you begin to realize that these people just want the same thing that we all want—food, housing, and a brighter future for their children. Many churches in the United States have declared themselves sanctuaries and do what they can to protect undocumented workers. But there is more work to be done. We need to repent of our complicity in turning away from refugees and migrants.

CONCLUDING REFLECTIONS

The third practice is *repentance*. This includes recognizing and repenting of our complicity in many sins. For example, we need to repent of the racism and sexism that characterize so much of the church and the world. This is difficult. We often don't see how we've contributed to this problem. In the United States there is real tension between Asian Americans and African Americans, which we'll get into in the chapter on reconciliation. I (Grace) as a Korean American have come to understand how we experience this racial tension and contribute to it.

We need to ask ourselves difficult questions. How have my attitudes and practices disadvantaged the elderly, Muslims, people of color, indigenous peoples, undocumented migrants or refugees, women, the poor, those with disabilities, or other groups? How have my choices and preferences and attitudes silenced and marginalized these groups? How do my political decisions compound the problem? Then, how do I repent and embrace the mind of Christ?

We'd like to offer one final example of repentance: repenting of the things we've either done to marginalize others or that contributed to their marginalization. The Gospel of Luke describes Jesus' concern for those marginalized in society. Jesus identifies with the outcast and himself was from the margins. Jesus welcomes, hears, and prioritizes the poor, the sinners, the women, the sick, the rejected, and the outcast. His concern for those on the margins is scandalous. It's in sharp contrast to the spirit of his age and to the nationalistic, uncompassionate religiosity of other religious leaders.

Jesus calls us to repent of the things we've done—and the attitudes we've harbored—that have served to marginalize others. Jesus calls us to welcome, embrace, and listen to those who are marginalized by society for a variety of reasons:

- those marginalized because of their physical life (including the disabled, the elderly, and the sick)
- those marginalized because of their race, ethnicity, or gender (including indigenous groups, people of color, and women)
- those marginalized because of their religion, profession, or sexual orientation (including Muslims, sex workers, and same-sex-attracted persons)
- those marginalized because of their political persuasions (including those who hold different political views from you)

In this process of repentance, we join Jesus in compassion, welcome, and friendship. Jesus welcomes to table fellowship those who are usually shunned. Jesus was crucified because of the people he ate with. Our repentance leads to us to the same table fellowship.

PRACTICES, CHALLENGES, AND ACTIVITIES FOR SMALL GROUPS

Here are some practices and activities for your small group. These will help you explore and experience the practice of repentance.

As we have noted, repentance is a four-stage process. Here are some actions that can help your small group explore these stages.

Conviction: Open to the conviction of the Holy Spirit. Conviction involves recognizing that one or more of our attitudes and behaviors are wrong. They are broken and sinful, and they damage us and others. Practice *conviction* together:

1. Pray as a group that God would fill your hearts with conviction.

2. Find ways to go into your neighborhoods and communities and to be with people marginalized because of their race, sexuality, politics, religion, disability, language, socioeconomic status, and so on. Some will be in your church, and others will not. As you spend time with and speak with them (individually and with your small group), what is the Holy Spirit convicting you to repent of?

3. Now, on large sheets of paper (or on a whiteboard), list the things that the Spirit is convicting you to repent of. These might come from the introductory sections or twelve points made in this chapter. Or the list that the Spirit leads your group to write may be completely different.

Contrition: Lament and mourn these things. Contrition involves lamenting and mourning our mistakes and sins, their effect on people and the earth, and their offensiveness to God. This is godly sorrow that moves us to action. So it is time to write another shared group lament. Practice *contrition* together:

1. Write a group lament as described in chapter two.

2. Choose one or more of the issues you wrote on your paper (or whiteboard) at stage one (*conviction*).

3. Then, following the nine elements of lament, spend some time in your small group writing a shared lament for the issues you chose. Write a lament together, structured around these nine stages or elements (described earlier): invocation, worship, description, connection, lament, confession, petition, trust, and praise. You might do this by asking people in pairs to write one or two of these nine stages or elements.

4. Spend time together in prayer over the themes in the lament. Open to the contrition that the Holy Spirit inspires.

Commitment: Commit to new and redemptive attitudes, postures, and behaviors. Commitment is about determining together to change our minds, attitudes, purpose, desires, and ways. We need to make this commitment together and rely on the power of the Holy Spirit. Practice *commitment* together:

1. Ask members of your small group to do the following before you meet next time:

   a. Consider the list that you have formed together of things you feel convicted to repent of.

   b. Individually during the week, write personal commitments to new, redemptive, God-honoring attitudes and behaviors on a piece of paper.

2. Share these commitments with each other next time you meet.

3. Give each other feedback on these commitments.

4. Spend time praying together that God would help you keep these commitments personally and as a group.

5. Do all this in a spirit of repentance, grace, forgiveness, love, faith, and hope.

Change: Practice becoming new in the world. Conviction, contrition, and commitment must lead to change. We start with recognizing what we have done. Then we move on to repentance, to
seeking justice for those whom we and others have wronged, and,
where appropriate, to acts of reparation. Reconciliation only happens
when we repent and seek justice, truth, freedom, and reparation. In
other words, reconciliation and forgiveness demand a new way of
being and living in the world (personally and together). Practice
change together:

1. Form three- or four-person accountability groups out of your
   small group. Invite people to choose whom they'd like to be in
   a small accountability group with.

2. This accountability group may meet separately from your
   normal group time. Or it may meet for accountability discussions for thirty minutes during your normal meeting times.

3. When groups meet, they should begin with prayer, recognizing
   that change only happens in community and through the
   grace and power of God. We can't orchestrate change (personally or in accountability groups). Only God gives us the
   power to change.

4. The group should also commit to confidentiality, empathy,
   prayer, listening, honesty, and being accountable to each other.

5. Now, in these accountability groups, discuss the list you have
   formed of things you feel convicted to repent of. Discuss the
   commitments you have made to change.

6. Hold each other accountable for actions that express this
   change. Ask each other tough questions about how you are
   changing your attitudes, postures, and behaviors. (For example: How are you letting go of the pursuit of power and
   control in your relationships? How are you dealing with racism,

sexism, and gender inequality in your life, ministry, and work-place? How are you listening to those who are different from you—sexually, politically, racially, religiously, and so on? How are you opening your heart to refugees and immigrants? How are you caring for the earth, the poor, the disabled, the margin-alized, and so on?)

FOUR

RELINQUISH POWER

To **relinquish something is** to voluntarily choose to give it up. The church will never truly be the new humanity in Christ until it embraces relinquishment. The gospel of Jesus Christ calls us to relinquish (to give up) our own righteousness, status, privilege, selfish ambition, self-interest, vain conceit, personal gain, and power.

Jesus practiced relinquishment, and Paul followed his example. In Philippians 2:5-11 Paul describes how Jesus emptied and humbled himself. Jesus chose the path of relinquishment, and we must embrace the same mindset. "In your relationships with one another, have the same mindset as Christ Jesus:

Who, being in very nature God,
did not consider equality with God something to be used to
his own advantage;
rather, he made himself nothing
by taking the very nature of a servant,
being made in human likeness.

And being found in appearance as a man,
he humbled himself

> by becoming obedient to death—
>> even death on a cross!" (Phil 2:5-8)

God exalted Jesus, but only after Jesus walked willingly down the path of self-emptying, humility, and relinquishment.

It isn't only in the incarnation that Jesus practiced relinquishment. He also relinquished status and power throughout his life. Consider, for example, John 4, where Jesus meets a Samaritan woman. Emmanuel Katongole observes, "Driven by fear, many Jews in Jesus' day made a point to walk around Samaria. . . . Jesus takes the most direct route right thru Samaria. Jesus gets tired and thirsty. He sits by the well and when a Samaritan woman (the enemy) comes to draw water he asks her for help 'Will you give me a drink?' He comes vulnerable into (so-called) enemy territory. He opens space."[1] Embracing vulnerability and powerlessness, Jesus asks the Samaritan woman for water. Jesus isn't just setting up a conversation about living water. He asks her for help. We often miss this. Jesus relinquishes his power to a woman of low racial and societal status, and in the process he changes the power dynamic between them. Brenda Salter McNeil writes, "In that instant he skillfully and profoundly empowers her to be the 'helper' and he becomes the 'helped.' Jesus has challenged the structural and personal alienation generated by their power differential. On the surface this may seem like a simple gesture, but upon closer inspection it becomes apparent that what Jesus has done is actually transformational!"[2]

After reflecting on the example of Jesus, Paul shares how he is also seeking to relinquish his own righteousness and power. Paul basically says, "If anyone should have confidence in their personal, moral, religious, and racial power, it's me." He was a "Hebrew of Hebrews" (Phil 3:5), in full possession of the covenantal, racial, and religious privileges that came with that. His ancestry and racial credentials were impeccable. Not only this, but he was a leading religious figure, outstanding even among his peers. He was religiously observant, spiritually zealous, personally ambitious, and, "as for righteousness based on the law, faultless" (Phil 3:6). But Jesus Christ has called him to relinquish all that, just as Jesus himself had relinquished his power.

Paul tells us what it means for him to practice relinquishment:

> But whatever were gains to me I now consider loss for the sake of Christ. What is more, I consider everything a loss because of the surpassing worth of knowing Christ Jesus my Lord, for whose sake I have lost all things. I consider them garbage, that I may gain Christ and be found in him, not having a righteousness of my own that comes from the law, but that which is through faith in Christ—the righteousness that comes from God on the basis of faith. I want to know Christ—yes, to know the power of his resurrection and participation in his sufferings, becoming like him in his death, and so, somehow, attaining to the resurrection from the dead. (Phil 3:7-11)

Paul relinquishes his personal, sexual, moral, religious, and racial power for the sake of Christ. He counts it all as loss, filth, and rubbish. Instead, following the example of Jesus, he lets all that go. It is only through relinquishing these things that he (and we) can know Christ. When we give up our power, we gain access to a new kind of power: the power of Jesus' resurrection and of participation in his sufferings.

For most of us, our power (or powerlessness) is found in our wealth, education, age, intellect, cultural capital, social standing, gender, profession, religious status, political access, ethnicity, and race. Power can be destructive and divisive. But it can also be healing and nurturing when it is released, when it is used for others' well-being and human flourishing. Henri Nouwen says that there is "the power that oppresses and destroys. . . . I want to show how that power is disarmed through powerlessness, and finally I want to proclaim the true power that liberates, reconciles, and heals."[3]

We relinquish power when we truly listen to those who've been marginalized. We receive from them as we genuinely listen to them and respond. We relinquish power (and we use what power we have for good) when we use all our energies to make sure the marginalized are heard, respected, honored, and responded to. We relinquish power when we seek to give power away and move the margins to a welcoming center—a multivoiced, multipeopled, multicultural, new creation, new humanity. We relinquish power when we say no to opportunities so that other voices can be heard. We relinquish power when we say yes to justice and action so that other voices can be honored.

We understand that justice, reconciliation, and healing cannot occur until we give power away. As James H. Cone says about racial power and reconciliation, "For white people to speak of reconciliation at the very moment that they are subduing every expression of black self-determination is the height of racist arrogance."[4] Reconciliation is only possible when the church takes on a different set of practices, habits, and postures.

RELINQUISHING POWER AND EMBRACING POWERLESSNESS

Henri Nouwen wrote a profound book on power and weakness. The lust for power corrupts the human spirit, damages relationships, perverts institutions, calcifies religions, destroys nature, entrenches inequalities, multiplies wars, and leads to all kinds of evil. God weeps. God calls his disciples to relinquish the lust for power and to embrace powerlessness. "In Jesus of Nazareth, the powerless God appeared among us to unmask the illusion of power. . . . God became human, in no way different from other human beings, to break through the walls of power in total weakness."[5]

Jesus showed us what it means to give away power. He calls us to relinquish power, to embrace powerlessness, and to give power to others (especially to those that the world has despised or denied power). Mother Teresa reminds us that Jesus came into this world for one purpose, and that is to show us he loves us. He did that by giving up his power and his life for us.[6]

There is power in the gospel and in Christ. But it is a power the world does not often understand. In weakness, foolishness, and vulnerability we discover a world-transforming power. In humility and self-giving we open space for God to reveal his power. It is the power of grace and love. It is the power of peace and integrity. It is the power of the Spirit and truth. It is the power that honors and heals, forgives, and unites. It is the power of giving power away.

RELINQUISHING RACIAL POWER

I (Graham) am the direct beneficiary of white privilege. I grew up in a working-class family in one of the poorest areas of Sydney. My grandfather didn't own a pair of shoes before joining the Australian Army to fight in the Second World War. Growing up among the workers of the banana plantations in northern New South Wales, my family was poor and rural. Wounded during the fighting in the jungles of Papua New Guinea, my grandfather returned to Australia to work menial-labor jobs his whole life. He never spoke about the horrors he experienced in the war, but at his funeral an Australian Army officer described how most of his battalion had been killed in the unspeakable violence that unfolded in those jungles. His son, my father, struggled to read and write, and he left school at an early age. My father was a truck driver, and my mother worked various retail jobs. Both left school when they were young and worked hard their whole lives to buy us a home and send us to a small private school in one of the poorest parts of Sydney.

But even with those struggles, I am still aware of the way I have benefited from white privilege. My grandfather and grandmother received government pensions for their military service in the Second World War. They also had government financial support in the areas of housing and health care. But the Aboriginal and Torres

Strait Islander soldiers who served alongside my grandparents—even those who were wounded—received nothing. Many did not receive a single dollar. More than four thousand Aboriginal men and women and 850 Torres Strait Islanders served in the war. They were pilots, sailors, soldiers, nurses, and more. But they were mostly forgotten after the war and were denied the financial, housing, and health care benefits given their white peers. Being former soldiers did not stop the Australian government from taking their children away from them.

My (Graham's) grandparents and parents worked hard at laboring and menial jobs to send us to a good school. I'm grateful for their effort and hard work! But I remember my Aboriginal childhood friends (I didn't have many Aboriginal friends when I was a boy, but I had a few). The fathers of my Aboriginal friends were often denied jobs and could never afford to send their children to the school that I went to. My father and mother managed to scrape together their dollars and buy us a home—a lovely little home that I spent my entire childhood in. But my Aboriginal friends often lived in terrible conditions, moving houses many times every year. While I had access to a private school, then university, and then enviable career prospects, the Aboriginal children I grew up with had none of those things. The system was rigged in my favor. The world was my oyster. White privilege had delivered me a good education, a stable home, and a host of opportunities. I loved my Aboriginal friends. But it doesn't matter whether I had racist thoughts or not—I am a direct beneficiary of white privilege. My society and culture gave me access to white power, while others around me were often robbed of prospects, dignity, their voices, and hope. I did nothing to deserve the power of my white privilege. My Aboriginal friends (and many people of color who grew up in my suburb) did nothing to deserve the discrimination and animosity and struggles they faced, often daily.

Ever since the colonial period, the gestalt of *whiteness* has ruled. What is whiteness? Whiteness includes skin color, but it's more than that. Whiteness is a way of seeing the world and of judging and ranking the people in it. Whiteness is about race, money, status, power, agency, desirability, and more. Whiteness is about where one falls on the scale between being "white" (seen as good, ideal, elect, beautiful, and desirable) and being "black" (seen as the opposite of those things). Whiteness leads to a racialized, displaced, and violent world. It has formed oppressive and mythical notions of "race." *White privilege* is an expression of a broader problem we're calling *whiteness*.

All of us are tempted to use our racial power in oppressive ways. This isn't just a European problem. We see racial violence and discrimination, for instance, among Asian and African peoples too. The desire to exert racial power over others is a global human problem.

How do we relinquish racial power? The first step is acknowledging that racism is fundamentally about *power*, *system*, and *agency*.[7] I (Graham) loved my Aboriginal childhood friends, and I respected and cherished them as much as my white friends. But while racial power, societal systems, and personal and cultural agency were readily available to me, these things were denied to them.

Racism is about the power to enslave, discriminate, oppress, punish, steal land, and define the rules. Racism is about the legal, religious, political, educational, and historical systems that entrench inequalities. And racism is about the denial of agency to those who are marginalized and silenced.

Racism has often led to a distorted understanding of self. Like a disease, it spreads throughout one's existence and can be undetected as it presents itself as a guise for how society exists in the Western world.[8] Thus racism needs to be defeated and eliminated from our culture, church, and society.

The second step is to find ways to give up our racial power. This isn't easy because this power is usually maintained through systems and institutions. But we need to make a conscious effort to give up power, to restore justice, to reactivate hospitality, to reinforce agency, to reconcile through repentance, and to recover life together. This will involve confronting institutionalized racism in church and society, and it will involve the kind of self-emptying and relinquishment modeled by Jesus Christ.[9] Jim Wallis says,

> We can no longer plead that we are unaware of the systems around us and what their consequences are for our fellow citizens and brothers and sisters of color. The way things are must no longer be accepted—especially by the dominant racial group that most benefits from that unfairness. Things must change, and a new generation must take up that task. White privilege is a sin of which we must repent, and the best way to show that is by changing practices and policies—and by helping to create new communities that provide for another way.[10]

RELINQUISHING OTHER FORMS OF POWER

Racial power isn't the only form of power that we need to relinquish. We must choose to relinquish other forms of power that corrupt our faith and witness, disempower others, and keep us from the counter-cultural, revolutionary power of Jesus Christ. Here we mention just a few of these forms of power.

We must relinquish political power. Too often Christians turn to political parties and personalities to achieve certain ends. We hold on to whatever political power we can muster in the hope to influence and shape society. But Stanley Hauerwas and Jonathan Tran remind us that this is a failure of Christian political imagination.

> It will serve Christians to remember that there are *many* ways to be political. Gathering with others around the given body of Christ, a *polis* through and through, is one such way, and is for Christians the original way. . . . To us the most troubling thing was not that Christians voted for Trump when they had plenty of reasons and ways not to do so. While regrettable, that mistake

follows a more basic one. We are most troubled by the ongoing belief Christians hold that the nation-state, not the church, is the arbiter of Christian political action. This belief obligates Christians to modes of statecraft in order to fulfill their moral commitments. In order to play at statecraft—again, for one's "vote to count"—Christians will have to prioritize those commitments that will survive the state's political processes over those that will not.[11]

The church is political. But its politic is not of this world.

We must also relinquish religious and theological power. Religion and theology have often been used to oppress, silence, and disempower. This is as true today as it was in Jesus' time. There are few things quite as insidious and damaging as the abuse of spiritual and religious power. The religion and theology that Jesus desires bring healing, life, freedom, and empowerment. Such faith and theology prioritizes the religious, theological, and spiritual expressions of those who are usually ignored and silenced. This is about giving away power and discovering the astonishing power within weakness.

We must relinquish linguistic power. English is a global language, but its use isn't always considered. Why do we have so many English-language theology and ministry texts translated into other languages instead of sponsoring books written in other languages? Scholars in Korea are expected to write an article in an English journal to gain "credibility" as a scholar in Korea. Why don't we give power away by encouraging people to do theology in their own language, by supporting people to write in their own languages, and by sponsoring the publication and distribution of non-English-language books?

We must relinquish gender-based power. Women experience discrimination and disadvantage on a daily basis. This is as true in the church as in other parts of society. It is time, especially for men, to give away their power so that women can flourish and experience life fully. Grace writes elsewhere,

Clearly, as women accept their call into ministry, many are experiencing prejudice and sexism. The problem is even more shameful as it relates to women of color clergy. Women of color are usually the last hired and the first fired for paid church and denominational positions. Women of color also are faring poorly in gaining jobs in theological education. Even those institutions that supposedly comprise people who are theologically trained, continue to discriminate against women of color!

Sunday morning is not only the most segregated day of the week, it is the day of week that women of color clergy are most discriminated against. What are we to do with this discrimination and prejudice that exist so prominently within the religious community? Are we to sit back, continue to throw our hands up in the air in exasperation, and give up hope for ourselves and for our daughters? Women clergy and those who support them are loudly saying "NO! This discrimination must end on our watch."[12]

EMBRACING THE POWER OF THE CROSS AND THE RESURRECTION

Jesus calls us to relinquish our power. He invites us to embrace a different kind of power—one rooted in powerlessness, weakness, and foolishness. After washing the disciples' feet Jesus asks them, "Do you understand what I have done for you?" (Jn 13:12). "Now that I, your Lord and Teacher, have washed your feet, you also should wash one another's feet. I have set you an example that you should do as I have done for you" (Jn 13:14-15). This astonishing and countercultural power is the power of the cross and resurrection. We find this power in empathy, repentance, relinquishment, humility, integrity, justice, equality, diversity, reconciliation, and life together.

In the summer of 2009 my (Grace's) mother was diagnosed with stage four lung cancer. The doctors gave her six months to live. As her daughter, I always thought my mother was not afraid of anything. But as soon as she was diagnosed, with tears gushing out, we all recognized that she was afraid. My mother was terrified of dying. Her fear continued through the last six months of her life. A close friend who was a minister came to the hospital to offer prayers for my mother. He wanted to pray alone with my mom, so he asked my sister and me to leave the hospital bed.

After some time he finished and said that we could all rejoin my mother. The minister had done some "self-emptying prayer." The minister prayed that my mother could empty herself and give up her power and allow the Spirit to come in. It was clear that my mother gave up her power and allowed the Spirit to move. She was finally at peace, and the fear was gone from her eyes. She passed away peacefully two weeks later.

There are many ways of giving up power and different kinds of power. Part of relinquishing our power, whatever it may be, is to surrender ourselves to the power of the Spirit, who moves us, empowers us, and gives us new life.

After giving everything up, Paul spoke of the power he discovered in Jesus Christ. This is the power of Jesus' resurrection. It is the power of "participation in his sufferings, becoming like him in his death, and so, somehow, attaining to the resurrection from the dead" (Phil 3:10-11).

Are you struggling to relinquish power for the sake of Christ and others? Paul talks of his own struggle to give all this up for the sake of Christ.

> Not that I have already obtained all this, or have already arrived at my goal, but I press on to take hold of that for which Christ Jesus took hold of me. Brothers and sisters, I do not consider myself yet to have taken hold of it. But one thing I do: Forgetting what is behind and straining toward what is ahead, I press on toward the goal to win the prize for which God has called me heavenward in Christ Jesus. (Phil 3:12-14)

Relinquishing power (and giving up our confidence in the flesh) isn't natural or easy. But the Spirit of Christ enables us.

PRACTICES, CHALLENGES, AND ACTIVITIES FOR SMALL GROUPS

Here is a small group simulation game to help your group think about relinquishing power. We have also offered a practice for conference and panel organizers and speakers. Both will help you embrace the practice of relinquishment.

Stop organizing all-white male panels and conferences, and stop speaking at them. If we are truly the church of Jesus Christ, why are we excluding so many groups from meaningful contribution? We can't tell you how often we look at a conference and panel lineup and think, "Where are the women speakers? And why on earth is this lineup so white?" Women and persons of color make up somewhere between 90 and 95 percent of the world's population. White men make up less than 10 percent (probably more like 6 percent).[13] So we are not talking about a small group in the population being ignored or marginalized in way too many conferences and panels. Are conference and panel organizers telling us that no one in that 90 to 95 percent of the global population has expertise or competence in the area the conference or panel is addressing? We don't believe it.[14]

Platform and panel speaking opportunities are chances to exercise power and influence. It is time to give this power away. So what can we do?

If you organize gatherings, conferences, or panels, please take this pledge: *I will not organize conferences or panels where all the speakers are male and white.* If you speak at gatherings, conferences, or panels, please take this pledge: *I will not speak at conferences or join in panels where all the speakers are male and white.*

Here are a few practical things we can do from here:

- Commit to developing a rich theology of diversity that deals with relevant biblical, theological, and missional themes. Commit to using the power you have to empower others (especially those who are usually denied opportunities).

- Make one (or both) of the pledges we're suggesting.

- Begin to develop a list of names of people of color and women who can speak at events.

- Make sure that women and people of color are involved in planning conferences, workshops, and panels. Make sure they are serving in positions of power and have equal access to attending the conference and building dynamic networks.

- If you're a conference organizer, work harder for diversity. Look for speakers at seminaries and local churches in order to make a commitment to increase diversity in the next four years. Without a real commitment and measurable goals, no change will happen.

- If you're a conference speaker, it's time to process whether you are willing to make the sacrifice of losing or sharing your spot for the sake of the church hearing another voice (there's always a danger when such change begins that we indulge in self-protection).

- Listen to the voices and concerns of women and people of color about this issue. How do they feel about what's been going on? How have they experienced marginalization, neglect, discrimination, and so on? How do they feel about the proposal we're making?

Take a "power audit." Mandy Marshall has designed a power audit that you can use in your small group. It will help you think about the power you have and use your power to confront injustices and the status quo. It will help you use power for the well-being of others. Take it at https://theglobalchurchproject.com/power/.

Get involved in grassroots organizations seeking to bring change to your neighborhood or community. We need to rethink our notions of power. Here's a way your small group can do this:

- Find grassroots organizations in your neighborhood or community that are seeking to bring positive change through the building of grassroots relational initiatives and actions to confront power that is authoritative, exploitative, self-serving, and so on. This is a kind of redistribution of power.

- Get involved with these groups (preferably over the long term), seeking to serve the communities they serve.

- Now, in your small group, talk together about what you are learning about power and its grassroots relational nature and redistribution.

Explore self-emptying power. Sarah Coakley has written a wonderful book called *Power and Submissions*. In it she explores the notions of vulnerability, self-emptying, and power. Coakley argues that there is power in self-emptying (there certainly was power in Christ's self-emptying) and that it confronts the abuse of power. Patterning our lives after Jesus' self-emptying (*kenosis*) enables us to unite human vulnerability with divine power—which confronts, subverts, and dismantles worldly and abusive visions and expressions of power. Vulnerability isn't weakness; it is an astonishing form of human strength.[15] Spend some time in your group discussing the following:

- How was the power of God revealed in Jesus' self-emptying and vulnerability?

- How does patterning our lives after Jesus' self-emptying (*kenosis*) enable us to unite our human vulnerability with God's divine power?

- Why does this "powerlessness" and vulnerability confront, subvert, and dismantle worldly and abusive visions and expressions of power? How does it do this?

- Together, pray for the courage to pursue a life of vulnerability, self-emptying, submission, and prayer. Pray for the strength to embrace the divine, grassroots, relational power that is found in vulnerability and that confronts the abuse of power.

FIVE

RESTORE JUSTICE

Misbah is thirteen, Shamin is seventeen, and Batol is ten. Misbah and Shamin fled Myanmar because of sexual and other violence. They are refugees, fleeing violence in the hope of safety and a better life. As of January 31, 2018, the Australian government has imprisoned Misbah on Christmas Island, and then on Nauru, for 1,648 days. Shamin has been imprisoned on Nauru for 1,559 days. Batol and her family fled Iran because of death threats and were sent by Australia to the Nauru detention center. As of January 31, 2018, Batol has been imprisoned on Nauru for 1,445 days.

As of January 31, 2018, close to forty children and their families are imprisoned on Nauru. These are children that Australia and the world have forgotten. These children are trapped in limbo, worn down by detention, and often self-harming. They suffer psychological and emotional damage, and they live in fear of the violence among the island's population. They struggle to hold on to any hope. They deserve freedom, hope, and a future. These children deserve justice.

On August 23, 2014, twenty-four-year-old Iranian asylum seeker Hamid Kehazaei, housed at the Manus Island offshore refugee processing center, sought treatment for an infected wound. The Australian government denied permission for him to be evacuated to the Australian mainland to receive medical treatment, which would have saved him. He died September 5, 2014. Hamid Kehazaei and his family deserve justice.

Comfort women were young Korean girls who were kidnapped or falsely promised work in factories only to be made into prostitutes by the Japanese imperial army from 1932 to 1945. Up to 400,000 women, mostly Korean, were taken to occupied territories to work as prostitutes serving up to one hundred men per night. A lot of these young women died of disease or by suicide. The few survivors never married and lived lonely lives because they were ashamed of what had happened to them. These women deserve justice.

Rosemary Brennan-Herrera spent nearly three years teaching children at the Manus Island offshore refugee processing center. It is one of two offshore Australian immigration detention centers, located at an old Australian Navy base in Papua New Guinea. In an article called "I Don't Understand How Such a Place Became Normal in the Australian Psyche," Brennan-Herrera describes the appalling conditions these refugee children and adults live in. She says, "What I saw was gratuitously cruel, insensitive and punishing. It was mortifying. It is Orwellian."

Brennan-Herrera then writes about the need for justice for these children. She says a day will come when they will be free, when dignity and justice will be restored.

It will end; it must end and you will have your lives back, your children back, your studies back and your professions back. I will never forget your ability to learn English in those conditions (and many taught it, as well), your astuteness, your resourcefulness, your many acts of kindness to me and your ability to find shared moments of pure joy amid the sadness; the raft, the cockatiels, the puppies, the cricket, the poetry, the cooking and the long conversations. . . . I truly hope we will be neighbours and friends into the future. You are certainly welcome at my house, anytime.[1]

Like many others, Misbah, Shamin, Batol, comfort women, and Brennan-Herrera long for a just world.

WHAT IS JUSTICE?

Justice is a central and complex biblical theme. The Bible presents God as a just God who calls for justice among his people, for creation, and in the world. We know what justice is when we know who God is. The just nature of God defines our understanding of justice. Micah 6:8 says,

> He has shown you, O mortal, what is good.
>   And what does the LORD require of you?
> To act justly and to love mercy
>   and to walk humbly with your God.

God requires all of us to engage in the work of justice.

Chris Marshall shows how this justice is most powerfully revealed in the person and work of Jesus Christ. "God's justice, incarnated in Jesus, is a liberating, community-creating power."[2] Jesus embodied the justice of God in his love, hospitality, truth, and grace. Jesus had a just mission. Revealing the justice of God, Jesus welcomed the stranger, rejected social discrimination, confronted economic injustice, spoke against institutional power, and repudiated war and violence. Standing in the tradition of the prophets, he showed a justice that was at once righteous and loving, ferocious and compassionate, uncompromising and gracious, visionary and personal, truth telling and forgiving, resolute and hospitable.[3] Jesus continues to show us today what justice means and how we can work toward justice.

Carol Dempsey says that the spirit of justice is "hospitality of heart." When we open our hearts to hospitality, we feel compelled to seek justice. When we embrace creation, the poor, our enemies, strangers, foreigners, outcasts, and others, we desire justice for them. We welcome without judging. We love our neighbors as ourselves. We reflect the justice, love, and hospitality of God. This hospitality leads us to desire and work for the flourishing, well-being, and good of others. Under President Trump, sanctuary churches are emerging to offer a safe place for immigrants who are in the country illegally. Rather than facing deportation, people are staying at sanctuary churches for protection. Providing such sanctuary is what it means to love our neighbor as ourselves.

Dempsey says that since "hospitality of heart" is the spirit of justice, then love for creation, the marginalized, the wronged, the poor, the disadvantaged, the disabled, the stranger, and the other is the work of justice. She says that compassion is the heart of justice; love and relationship are the wellsprings of justice; and peace is the flower (or fruit) of justice.

Finally, Dempsey says, justice is both an invitation and a vocation. It is God's invitation to hospitality, compassion, and peace. It is an invitation "to act justly and to love mercy and to walk humbly with your God" (Mic 6:8). And it is a profound, lifelong, and communal vocation—a calling to be a just people who reflect the love and hospitality of a just God.[4]

Danielle Strickland speaks of the biblical triangle of faith, mercy, and justice. She writes,

> Our relationship with God could be described as a triangle of faith, mercy (or peace) and justice. Scripture does not present them as competing aspects, or suggest that one flows out of the other; rather, they are a triangle that forms the basis of our relationship with God. Each text [Mic 6:8; Mt 23:23; Rom 14:17]

places justice or righteousness first on the list. Justice is not an optional extra. *It is our first activity.* Justice is the first and primary demand that God places on his people. As a God of justice (or righteousness), he expects that we, his community, be his agents for bringing justice to bear in the world; to usher in a just society without discrimination and with fair treatment and equality for all.[5]

We have seen that God is a just God who hates injustice. Injustice is a contagious sin that breaks and angers the heart of God. God's antidote to injustice is truth, love, grace, reconciliation, peace, compassion, and welcome.

God calls the church to be a just church. Our vocation is to be a just community that pursues justice for all peoples and all creation by acting justly, loving mercy, and walking humbly with our God.

WHAT DOES IT MEAN TO RESTORE JUSTICE?

Restoring justice involves educating ourselves about injustices in our neighborhood, society, and world. We must also educate ourselves about what it means to be a good and just neighbor for those exploited, on the margins, or suffering injustice.

Restoring justice involves talking openly and honestly about issues. Talk about injustices, deaths, discrimination, and atrocities. Talk about the lives and humanity of black and white and other people. Talk with people from across the spectrum—black and white, old and young, poor and rich, indigenous and nonindigenous, women and men.

Restoring justice involves listening to the concerns and perspectives of others even when these seem to address issues that don't directly affect us. It involves standing up for the rights and well-being of others—even if their well-being or prosperity or flourishing seems only indirectly related to ours, and even when their well-being comes at our expense.

This is about walking in other people's shoes. It's about addressing contemporary and historical injustices on behalf of others. We imitate the one who came into this world for our well-being—giving up his comfort, safety, power, and position. We follow the one who was wounded, bruised, rejected, and crucified for us. We imitate the one who restores justice in an unjust world.

Restoring justice also involves speaking and acting for justice. The Women's March in 2017 tried to do this as it engaged in speaking about and raising injustices that occur to women: equal pay, physical assault, discrimination, and so on. Restoring justice means addressing injustice head-on. This includes addressing systemic and structural injustices. Sympathy must move to compassion, which must move to love, which must move to advocacy and action. Love without action is meaningless. Compassion without justice is hollow. Solidarity without advocacy is only half the picture.

We must not be silent in the face of poverty, exploitation, injustice, sexism, racism, misogyny, torture, hate, division, conflict, and authoritarianism. We must choose to speak and act even when we know we will suffer the consequences. This means speaking out on Black Lives Matter, poverty, climate change, war, consumption and consumerism, health issues, nuclear weapons, the Palestine/Israel conflict, white privilege, sexism, racism, systemic and structural evils, and more. Dr. Larycia Hawkins lost her job at Wheaton College because she wore a hijab and wanted to stand in solidarity with Muslim brothers and sisters.[6]

Silence speaks volumes. When you or I choose not to act, we are in fact taking a form of action. We witness to Jesus and his kin-dom in our life together and in our risky, prophetic, and just words and actions.

Restoring justice involves prioritizing the well-being and human flourishing of the poor, wronged, marginalized, and disadvantaged. This only happens when we prioritize and value their agency and voice, and when we redistribute power and resources.

Restoring justice is fundamentally about following a just God and being a just church. God hates injustice. God is just. The biblical story is one of a just and loving God reaching out to humanity to restore justice, wholeness, healing, and redemption. The church is an alternative community. God calls this church to embrace, proclaim, embody, and practice restored justice. We do this by practicing a restored ethic, a restored hope, a restored community, a restored peace, a restored truth, a restored love, and a restored reconciliation.

OPENING OUR HEARTS TO THE SUFFERING OF OTHERS

As Christians we need to educate ourselves about justice and injustice. This begins by asking critical questions of ourselves, our churches, and our culture, and responding courageously to the answers.

What is justice? What causes injustice? What biblical and theological themes are relevant? What does Jesus say about justice and injustice? How do people experience injustice, and what does it do to their lives, families, and communities? How has the church been complicit in injustice? How have our theologies facilitated the exploitation of indigenous and First Nations peoples? In what ways have these theologies accelerated and enabled the plundering and warming of the earth? How has the church's posture and attitude entrenched divisions along ethnic, gender, and class lines? How can we acknowledge our sin and our complicity? What does it look like for the church to lament, repent, change, and seek forgiveness, justice, and reconciliation? What role does the church play in restoring justice? How is injustice expressed in racism, sexism, poverty, ecological degradation, war, debt, and so on? How can we—called by our just God to be a just church—help address these injustices and restore true justice?

But we will never understand injustice and justice until we open our hearts and lives to the suffering of others. John Dear tells the story of Oscar Romero. In the early years of his ministry as a priest he was not especially interested in the lives and plight of the poor. But when Romero became archbishop, he was challenged by Salvadorian Jesuit priest Rutilio Grande to learn from the poor. Grande challenged Romero to enter the lives of the poor, to listen to their suffering, to see injustices, and to speak on their behalf.

On March 12, 1977, Rutilio Grande was murdered for speaking up for the poor. Standing over Grande's dead body that night, Romero decided to give his life to championing the cause of the poor, suffering, and oppressed. He challenged the government and military, and he spoke out against the torture, disappearances, murders, and injustices suffered by the Salvadorian people.

Opening his heart to the suffering of others, Romero opened the seminary in downtown San Salvador to hundreds of homeless, hungry, and fearful people. He halted construction on a new cathedral in San Salvador and diverted the funds into programs to feed the hungry, clothe the poor, shelter the homeless, and educate children.

Eventually Romero was martyred for his work with and on behalf of the poor and oppressed. He opened his heart to the suffering of others and refused to be silent about injustice.

> Romero would drive out to city garbage dumps to look among the trash for the discarded, tortured victims of the death squads on behalf of grieving relatives. "These days I walk the roads gathering up dead friends, listening to widows and orphans, and trying to spread hope," he said. In particular, Romero took time every day to speak with dozens of people threatened by government death squads. People lined up at his office to ask for help and protection, to complain about harassment and death threats, and to find some support and guidance in their time of grief and struggle. Romero received and listened to everyone. His compassionate ear fueled his prophetic voice.[7]

Romero truly opened his heart to the suffering of others and understood what it meant to work for justice.

ADDRESSING INJUSTICE

God calls his people to stand for justice. This involves addressing historical, personal, systemic, and contemporary injustices. It includes
embracing and living a different and just way.

Addressing injustice requires understanding how race, gender,
class, and ability relate to one another. People suffer oppression
and injustice through the intersection of these. They aren't just
connected; they also compound and magnify one another. They
are bound together. The intensity of the injustice and oppression
one faces very often depends on how these things intersect in one's
life. Here's one example: a poor black woman is going to experience racism and sexism differently from a middle-class white
woman. To address injustice, Christians need to consider these
things carefully. This is a prophetic way of being in the world. It is
an approach to justice that begins in the intersections between a
person or group's ethnicity and their class and gender. It then
moves toward liberation and justice for all people inclusive of all
their differences. Kimberlé Crenshaw, a law professor, identifies
this phenomenon as "intersectionality."[8]

> Crenshaw explains intersectionality through this story from the
> courts. In DeGraffenreid v. General Motors, a group of Black
> women sued the company alleging discrimination against
> Black women in the company's seniority system. The court
> found against the women. Because General Motors could show
> that it had hired women (white women), the plaintiffs could not
> show that the company had discriminated on the basis of
> gender. The court recommended the women join another case
> alleging racial discrimination, but the plaintiffs refused because
> this recommendation overlooked that their claim alleged both
> race and sex discrimination. The court, nonetheless, refused to
> acknowledge Black women as a special class.[9]

As Christians we must recognize how power works across multiple forms of difference. This includes acknowledging that oppressive powers cannot be isolated or examined separately from one another. Rather, we must pay attention to the ways social differences give shape to one another. We must demand that remedies to discrimination and oppression also attend to the way injustices compound when issues of race, class, and gender overlap.

Religion as a social institution is not exempt from this. Religion often plays a role in maintaining hierarchies of power. Christianity specifically has been a key player in reproducing systems of oppression throughout history. It has done this through its support for the domination of women, imperialism, capitalism, slavery, and segregation. In recent years Christians have misused Scripture and theology to maintain social inequality. Most recently, many Christians have supported anti-woman, anti-immigrant, anti–people of color, and anti-poor policies.

Chung Hyun Kyung, who teaches at Union Theological Seminary in New York, says that the Bible needs to come with a warning label. We all know that cigarettes come with a warning label stating that smoking can cause lung cancer, heart disease, and emphysema. Chung says that the Bible's warning label should state that reading the Bible without guidance may lead to war, patriarchy, colonialism, slavery, classism, racism, and so on.

We cannot address injustice without attending to race, sexual identity, social class, ability, gender identity, and age. We cannot develop racial/ethnic theologies that do not attend to gender and sexual identity. When we create a singular identity as normative, we marginalize the intersections of diverse people within a group, who experience oppressions in varying ways because of the intersections.

Justice requires us to move toward dignity, hope, and freedom for all people inclusive of all their differences. Justice requires that we leave no one out. We must leave no one's experience unconsidered in exploring and expanding our ideas of God, sin, redemption, and the church. We must leave no one's oppression unchallenged and no system of oppression intact.

In our present political climate we will only address injustice if we think and act in a way that addresses how race, class, gender, and ability relate to one another and intensify one another. As the church we must resist institutions and ideologies that perpetuate oppression. We must care for the "least of these." In doing so we position the church not as a complicit institution but as a leader in a vision toward God's kin-dom that welcomes, affirms, encourages, and supports all of God's children in all their God-given complexity.

In this way the church seeks to restore justice to all people of all ethnicities, classes, and genders. So often Christians are so concerned about personal piety that they forget that God cares about the social conditions that we find ourselves in. We see this throughout the Bible. God was concerned about the social condition of the Israelites who were slaves in Egypt, the poor who lived under the Roman Empire, and the lepers who were outcasts in society. God cares about the social condition that we are in, and thus so should the church. In doing so we witness to the righteousness and liberation of our just God.

SPEAKING AND ACTING FOR JUSTICE

Brenda Salter McNeil has written a brilliant book on helping communities move toward wholeness and justice. It's called *Roadmap to Reconciliation*. In her book McNeil uses the acronym CARE to describe how we should do justice. These four steps move us out of inaction and get us involved in speaking and acting for justice.

Step one: Communicate. "The first step is to *communicate* what we have learned about a specific reconciliation or justice issue."[10] Silence perpetuates injustice. We must speak up when we see injustice happening in churches, workplaces, campuses, and anywhere else in society. This involves providing platforms for voices that are often silenced (women, indigenous peoples, people of color, minorities, etc.) to be heard. It involves being courageous and choosing to speak up against injustice.

Step two: Advocate. "Then we must *advocate* for change. . . . Talking isn't enough. We have to get moving."[11] This includes voting and marching for justice and addressing corporate and institutional injustices. It involves using the power we possess to work for justice in a wide range of areas. But it's also about advocating for justice close to home. It involves seeking to change injustices in your church and family and neighborhood.

Step three: Relate. We need to be a part of a community that is committed to reconciliation and that holds us accountable. We need partnerships with people whose ethnicity, gender, sexuality, ability, and socioeconomic status are different from ours.

Step four: Educate. Finally, McNeil says that we need to keep educating ourselves throughout our lives. McNeil says that teaching others to use CARE is a way we get involved in education.

Jesus calls his church to speak and act for justice. This is justice for the poor, for women, for minorities, for migrants, for the earth, for the sexually abused, for people of color, and more. To do this well we need to enter partnerships with others who also seek justice. We need collaborations for justice.

COLLABORATING FOR JUSTICE

Restoring justice is collaborative work. It only happens when we form courageous, surprising, and unified partnerships.

These partnerships happen at a local level when we join with others in our neighborhood to address local issues. Recently the state government decided to expand the freeway near my (Graham's) house. Many of our neighbors were visibly distressed by the construction noise, sleepless nights, dirt and dust, and glare of the floodlights. After twelve months, tired of watching my neighbors suffer, I gathered a small group of neighbors together to go door to door asking people to sign a petition demanding more consideration for the people of this neighborhood. We lobbied every influential person and group we thought might be interested or might have some stake or involvement in this construction. We wrote to local, state, and federal politicians, expressing our concerns and requests. As a result the corporation contracted by the government to expand the freeway offered compensation and housing relocation for those most affected by the construction noise. Our neighbors had collaborated for the sake of justice.

Partnerships also happen at a national and global level. Take the Sustainable Development Goals, for example.[12] These offer quantified and time-bound targets to address hunger, poverty, education, gender equality, child mortality, maternal health, environmental sustainability, disease prevention and cure, and more. Goal 17 stresses the importance of developing global partnerships. For the sake of the world's most vulnerable people, we need to encourage more and more national and global partnerships. Governments, businesses, nonprofits, religious organizations, and other groups need to collaborate for justice.

COMBINING JUSTICE WITH PEACE, BEAUTY, RECONCILIATION, AND LOVE

Sometimes we think of justice as a harsh or cold thing. Maybe that's because we often associate it with judges and legal systems. But justice is beautiful. Justice draws together mercy, humility, beauty, compassion, and love. Cornel West puts it this way: "To be human you must bear witness to justice. Justice is what love looks like in public— to be human is to love and be loved."[13]

When justice prevails the world is a more peaceful, beautiful, reconciled, and loving place. This is a taste of the age to come. We look forward to the age when God will replace war, famine, disease, racism, sexism, and the like with peace, plenty, diversity, inclusion, beauty, reconciliation, love, and justice. Creation and humanity groan for this day. This justice is our hope and vision. Justice is beautiful, and through God's justice and love, God restores all things. It is beautiful to see trees being planted to replenish the earth, it is beautiful to see a refugee living in her new home, and it is beautiful to see a wrongly convicted man set free. Justice brings beauty and life.

RECEIVING AND OFFERING FORGIVENESS AND EMBRACE

Miroslav Volf says, "Forgiveness is an element in the process of reconciliation, a process in which the search for justice is an integral and yet subordinate element."[14] In this he means that *forgiveness* and *embrace* are at the heart of Christian faith and certainly at the heart of reconciliation and justice.

There is no forgiveness and reconciliation apart from justice. Forgiveness and reconciliation don't only occur after complete justice has been done (after all, justice is rarely, if ever, entirely satisfied in this life).

What is the idea at the heart of Volf's proposal? It is simply this: following the way of Christ, Christians seek both justice and reconciliation, and they do this through the will to embrace the other and through actual embrace. This isn't cheap grace. But it is offering forgiveness and embrace while justice is pursued, even when justice hasn't been completely fulfilled. We choose to offer forgiveness and embrace as an act of grace and while we seek justice. This is risky. It involves self-denial and unconditional love. This forgiveness doesn't stand apart from justice but is offered regardless of whether such justice is complete.

When someone offers us this forgiveness and embrace, our response is to repent for what we have done wrong, to offer restitution, and to embrace and forgive in return. This is the way of the cross. It's a difficult, risky, and often painful way. But this will to embrace—and actual embrace—unifies forgiveness, reconciliation, and justice.[15]

PRACTICES, CHALLENGES, AND ACTIVITIES FOR SMALL GROUPS

Here are some practices and activities for your small group. These will help you embrace the practice of restoring justice.

Learn about a biblical theology of justice. Spend four weeks reading and discussing Chris Marshall's *The Little Book of Biblical Justice.* Discuss these and other questions: What do we learn about justice from the biblical text? Why is justice a central theme in the Bible? How does our understanding and practice of justice arise out of God's just nature and actions? What are the key contours of biblical justice? How do we live out biblical justice, individually and as a group? What did Jesus teach us about justice? How can we reject social discrimination? How can we address economic, gender, and racial injustices? How can we identify and change injustices in (and supported by) the church and its theology? What does the Bible say about a just approach to war and violence (and peace and nonviolence)? How does the new messianic community confront injustice and embody and proclaim God's justice (following the life and example of its Messiah)?

Write prayers about justice (and about peace and reconciliation). Having thought about a biblical theology of justice, now spend an evening writing prayers about justice. You might also write prayers about peace, forgiveness, and reconciliation. Try writing both individual prayers and a group prayer.

Collect and sing worship songs that focus on justice. You will want to collect your own list of songs, but here are some examples: "Compassion Hymn" by Stuart Townsend, "Justice" by Andreana Tait, "God of Justice" by Tim Hughesk, "Beauty for Brokenness" by Graham

Kendrick, "O God, You Call for Justice" by Carolyn Winfrey Gillette, and "More Than Songs" by Stephen Miller. (You may even choose to write your own song about justice.)

Write a series of justice commitments, and hold each other accountable for being justice advocates. Here's what to do in your small group:

- *Write a series of justice commitments.* These will be twenty things you commit to do (individually and together) to address injustice by changing your own personal and group behaviors. You will have five commitments in each of these four categories: racial justice, gender justice, economic justice, and environmental justice.

- *Hold each other accountable for keeping these commitments.* You are keeping each other accountable to be justice advocates. You are each seeking to change parts of your daily lives, to lessen the suffering of others, to avoid creating more injustice, and to bring justice.

Go to a justice conference together. We all need to be inspired and informed by others who are seeking justice in this world. Go to a conference together such as The Justice Conference, the Beyond Festival, or Voices for Justice.[16] Spend time after the conference debriefing about how you will respond to what you've seen and heard.

Support groups working for justice. Find out which groups in your neighborhood, city, or country are working for justice (and to transform communities and neighborhoods). Choose one or two that particularly challenge you. Now ask them how you can support them (and get involved in their work) as a small group. There are thousands of groups that you can choose from. One example is the Christian Community Development Association.[17]

Make lifestyle changes that reflect the UN's Sustainable Development Goals. The United Nations offer a helpful little list of things you and your group can do to help the world reach the Sustainable Development Goals. Here's how they introduce this guide:

> End extreme poverty. Fight inequality and injustice. Fix climate change. Whoa. The Global Goals are important, world-changing objectives that will require cooperation among governments, international organizations and world leaders. It seems impossible that the average person can make an impact. Should you just give up? No! Change starts with you. Seriously. Every human on earth—even the most indifferent, laziest person among us—is part of the solution. Fortunately, there are some super easy things we can adopt into our routines that, if we all do it, will make a big difference. We've made it easy for you and compiled just a few of the many things you can do to make an impact.[18]

The guide is available at un.org/sustainabledevelopment/takeaction.

SIX

REACTIVATE HOSPITALITY

In the southwestern area of Sydney is one of Australia's most rapidly growing and ethnically diverse churches. Parkside Baptist Church consists of people from over fifty different linguistic, cultural, and ethnic backgrounds. They gather as one family for worship and mission, reflecting a united, diverse congregation of Christian faith. Their dream is to become a vibrant congregation from more than one hundred different ethnic backgrounds, worshiping together as one family, affecting Australia and beyond. They desire "to be a Christian community committed to sharing Christ with people of all nations."[1]

Surrounding the walls of Parkside Church are the flags of these fifty nations. Thirty percent of Parkside's congregation are from an Anglo-Celtic background. Forty percent are first-generation migrants to Australia. The other 30 percent are second- or third-generation Australians from migrant families.

Parkside's mission in southwestern Sydney includes a program called Just Care. This is a community outreach of Parkside. It provides practical help and support to disadvantaged youth, children, and families from diverse ethnicities and religions in their area.

Parkside is located in a melting pot of cultures and ethnicities. It's one of the first places migrants settle when they arrive in Australia. Since its inception Parkside's Just Care has provided emergency food parcels, financial assistance, and job training to people in the local community. A Just Care trailer equipped with barbecue facilities has been visiting local parks to contact youth and families and to share the gospel. Parkside congregants teach English to new migrants. They welcome them to Australia and into their lives, families, church, and homes.

Aside from its mission within Sydney, Parkside has international mission teams serving among the world's poorest. They especially serve in Asia and the Indian subcontinent. The church's passion for mission among all the nations and ethnicities of Australia and the Asia-Pacific is becoming truly global as its people seek to reflect the Messiah's love for all the peoples of the world.

We need more churches like Parkside Baptist Church. This is especially the case as our cities become increasingly multicultural and multiethnic. Recently I (Graham) have been involved in discussions about a new church plant in western Sydney. A team of Africans, North Americans, and Australians are working together to set up a multicultural church plant there. The pastor of that plant will most likely be Kenyan. The leadership team will be made up of women and men from many parts of the globe.

HOSPITALITY, THE PAST, AND A CHANGING WORLD

London, Paris, New York, and Sydney are astonishingly diverse cities. But other cities, regional towns, and rural areas are rapidly becoming multicultural, multiethnic, and multilingual too. Seoul, Korea, where I (Grace) was born, was relatively homogeneous until very recently. Now there are many other south Asians, east Asians, Africans, and white people living in Korea. In time Korea will become more diverse with migrant workers, intermarriages, and immigration.

Diversity, of course, isn't limited to language and ethnicity. Our cities are melting pots of religions, worldviews, sexualities, and lifestyles. The world is changing, and our cities and rural areas are changing. The world is only going to become more diverse and pluralistic due to immigration, refugees, and globalization. Climate change is now creating climate refugees, who are fleeing their countries due to loss of farmland, extreme temperatures, or unlivable conditions due to severe storms and weather patterns. This presents interesting and also wonderful opportunities for church and mission. It presents an amazing opportunity for the church to be the new humanity in Jesus Christ.

Jim Wallis, Willie James Jennings, J. Kameron Carter, Brenda Salter McNeil, Christena Cleveland, and others have helped us see how the church has shaped its theological and social imagination around racism, sexism, and fear of diversity (fear of the other). They have helped us think about how to rectify this and embrace the other.[2] They call us to repentance, justice, and reconciliation. They call us to a different, transformative, diverse way of being the people of God in the world. They challenge us to reactivate the practice of hospitality.

The world is rapidly changing. Instead of responding with fear, we can embrace hope, love, and renewal. We can choose to be a people of every nation, and tribe, and people, and tongue. We can choose to worship as one body, the one who calls women and men together from every nation in every part of the globe. We can be hospitable.

HOSPITALITY AND THE NEW HUMANITY

In chapter one we outlined the biblical vision for the new humanity in Jesus Christ. New-humanity churches embrace the diversity of the body of Christ. They embrace this fully, not in a partial or tokenistic way. They welcome diversity in its many forms. They grasp the importance of ethnic, linguistic, cultural, gender, racial, socioeconomic, and theological diversity.

New-humanity churches know that they are one body. As a diversity-in-unity people, they have one Messiah, one Spirit, one life, one table, one politic, one righteousness, one peace, one mission, one faith, one hope, and one love.

The local and global Christian community is stunningly diverse. It is 2.2 billion people, united together in love and through the gospel of Jesus Christ. Bruce Milne puts it this way:

> What contrasts of race and ethnicity are here! What ranges of generation and gender, language and culture, customs and worship styles, social status and wealth indices, education levels and forms of employment; what degrees of freedom, involving in some places intrusive restrictions and even persecution; what varieties of personal faith stories, and levels of comprehension and commitment! Yet all that incredible diversity has a single, authentic point of unity: Jesus Christ. In the supernatural reality of his risen presence through the Holy Spirit, the multi-faceted community is *one* as his body on earth. In Jesus they are *one* people, *one* life.[3]

He continues,

> Here is the great Ephesian image of the church. It is a new humanity, a community consisting of people remade. This is, I believe, the supreme image for our time, both for the church universal and for the church local. . . . [In Ephesians 2:11-18 the apostle Paul] is asserting nothing less than a *sheer creative action of God*. . . . [The creation of this new-humanity church] is a prodigy, a wonder, brought about by a supernatural, divine intervention, and hence a divine attestation to the gospel.[4]

When we posted this quote on Facebook, our friend Mark DeYmaz responded in this way:

> Certainly, a beautiful thought and sentiment. That said, I agree only in so far as this reality is intentionally expressed

in authentic, tangible ways via the unity and diversity of a local church. Otherwise, the wondrous, beautiful, diversity of the universal church, and subsequent proclamation of the gospel, i.e., a credible witness of God's love for all people, is unintentionally undermined when and wherever systemically (unnecessarily) segregated churches stubbornly remain the status quo. In an increasingly diverse and cynical society, those without Christ view ethnically segregated churches as if each worship its own god as expressed in its own desires and likeness . . . no different than 2,000 or 3,000 years ago when the Hittites had their gods, the Phoenicians had their gods, the Egyptians had their gods, and the Jews had their god. . . . If (since) the kingdom of heaven is not segregated, local churches on earth, wherever possible, should not be either.[5]

We agree. This new humanity in Christ is first expressed in tangible ways in the diversity in unity of the local, multiethnic church.

New-humanity churches make at least four important commitments. First, they move away from ethnic segregation and foster diverse, multiethnic, or intercultural churches. As DeYmaz says, this diverse, multiethnic, new-humanity church was envisioned by Christ (Jn 17:20-23), described by Luke (Acts 11:19-26; 13:1), and prescribed by Paul (Ephesians).[6] What a thrilling community to be a part of in this age and in the age to come! DeYmaz says that multiethnic churches have seven core commitments.

1. They depend on the Spirit to help them be a diverse, multi-ethnic, new humanity in Christ Jesus.

2. They take intentional steps to be multiethnic.

3. They empower diverse leaders.

4. They develop crosscultural relationships.

5. They pursue crosscultural competence, including cultural intelligence.

6. They promote a spirit of inclusion.

7. They mobilize for impact.[7]

We encourage you to read Mark DeYmaz's books on building multiethnic churches. You can find a list of his books at markdeymaz.com.

Second, new-humanity churches foster cultural intelligence (often abbreviated as CQ) among their leadership and in their congregation. Cultural intelligence is the ability to understand different cultures and function effectively in situations of cultural diversity. The Cultural Intelligence Center says that cultural intelligence requires four skills: (1) CQ drive: a passion and confidence to adapt to multicultural settings; (2) CQ knowledge: an understanding of the similarities and differences between cultures; (3) CQ strategy: planning for multicultural conversations, relationships, and interactions; and (4) CQ action: seeking out multicultural relationships, and adapting when relating and working interculturally.[8]

Third, new-humanity churches commit to welcoming, fostering, and relishing diversity in all its forms: gender diversity, socioeconomic diversity, theological diversity, physical diversity, ethnic diversity, and so on. They are hospitable.

Fourth, new-humanity churches are led by people who are committed to diversity and hospitality. These are lifelong learners about such things as leading multicultural teams, building multiethnic churches, and doing mission and ministry in pluralistic, diverse situations. This is transformative leadership. It refuses to accept the status quo. It is satisfied with nothing less than a diverse congregation and leadership team that fully reflects the new humanity in Jesus Christ.

HOSPITALITY AND BEING A GLOBAL CHURCH

One of the reasons we must embrace diversity is that we are a part of a global church. The shape and make-up of this global church is rapidly changing. Majority World, indigenous, and diaspora (immigrant) churches are redefining twenty-first century Christianity.[9] We are part of a diverse, global Christian community, and those of us who are Western Christians must decide how we'll respond.[10]

Philip Jenkins has predicted that "by 2025 fully two-thirds of Christians will live in Africa, Latin America, and Asia.... Scholars are fairly unanimous in acknowledging the accuracy of the facts. The 'average Christian' today is female, black, and lives in a Brazilian favela or an African village."[11] The church needs to wake up to this new growing reality. China is an example of the phenomenal growth of the church outside the West. If current rates of growth continue, within one generation China will have more Christians than any other nation on earth.

Jenkins concludes,

> We are currently living through one of the transforming moments in the history of religion worldwide. Over the last five centuries, the story of Christianity has been inextricably bound up with that of Europe and European-derived civilizations overseas, above all in North America. Until recently, the overwhelming majority of Christians have lived in white nations.... Over the last century, however, the center of gravity in the Christian world has shifted inexorably away from Europe, southward, to Africa and Latin America, and eastward, toward Asia. Today, the largest Christian communities on the planet are to be found in those regions.[12]

As the church grows in these different regions, the church needs to do things differently.

What does all this mean for the mission, theology, worship, and communities of the church worldwide? What does it mean especially for the Western church? How do we embrace this global diversity with relish?

I (Graham) interviewed missiologist Lamin Sanneh of Yale Divinity School for The GlobalChurch Project.[13] In that interview

Sanneh offered a striking challenge to the Western church. Here's our paraphrase of what he said: We in the West are a confident and articulate people. Theology has served us well as a vehicle of our aspirations, desires, and goals. There is no shortage of theological books on all sorts of imaginable subjects. There are how-to manuals instructing us about effective ministry. These manuals tell us how to fix our emotions. They affirm our individual identity and promote our choices and preferences. They tell us how to change society by political action. They show us how to raise funds and build bigger churches. They teach us to invest in strategic coalitions.

All this language leaves us little time or space to listen to God. What if God has something else to say to us? What if that something else challenges what we want to hear? Are we going to turn the other way, or are we going to be open to new challenges? Yet, without reciprocity in the moral and spiritual life, of hearing and responding to the intimations of the Spirit, it is hard to see how God can be salient in the lives of modern men and women.

The gospel suffers from a form of cultural captivity in the West. But the renewal of world Christianity has lessons to teach us all. The de-Westernization of Christianity may, if we allow it, help us address the Western cultural captivity of the gospel. Thanks to the grace and power and sovereignty of the Spirit of Christ, this de-Westernization of the global church may help us find freedom from our cultural captivity. The astonishing growth and vitality of movements in world Christianity will make this truth even more evident to us over the following decades.

We are a global church. We must commit to diversity and multiethnicity. We are enriched by indigenous, Western, diaspora, and Majority World voices. We gain new insight and depth from diverse voices, which all contribute to a deeper understanding of a God who loves us all.

We need a new narrative and a new way of telling our stories of God in our lives. The vast majority of the global church today isn't white, Western, and middle class. And the astonishing growth of world Christianity isn't happening in those places. It's happening in cultures outside the West. It's happening among women and children and people of color. Where there is growth and vitality in Western settings, it's usually among diaspora and immigrant churches. As Stephen Bevans says: today, the average Christian is female, a person of color, and living in Africa or Asia. We need a new, local-global, multiethnic, and diverse narrative.[14]

We must turn to the churches of Majority World and indigenous and diaspora cultures. Christians in these cultures help us rediscover what it means to be salt, light, and a city. They invite us into local-global conversations. To do this we, as Western Christians, must enter conversations with Majority World and diaspora and indigenous Christians. They have much to teach us. Listening to others helps us grow in our understanding and practice of mission and church and theology. We need to understand the new theologies that are emerging in the growing churches in the Global South. Neglecting or ignoring these voices will only perpetuate imperialistic Western domination. For far too long, we've been Eurocentric and Americentric. We've marginalized or ignored Majority World, diaspora, and indigenous voices.

New Majority World voices are rising and redefining our understandings of theology and church and mission. Many Majority World and diaspora and indigenous churches have extraordinary missional and theological vitality. Openness to these voices needs to happen now. It's time for Western churches, theologies, and mission to mature. Only through global conversations and exchanges can they reflect God's global mission.

Our hope is that over the coming decades we'll listen to the thoughts and practices of African, Asian, Pacific Islander, Caribbean, Eastern European, Oceanian, Middle Eastern, Latin American, First Nation, and indigenous thinkers. These dare us to examine our theologies and missions and churches. They inspire us to renew the worship and community and mission of Jesus' church. They stir us to think in fresh ways about what it means to be salt, light, and a city. They help us become a diverse church—a truly global church.[15]

HOSPITALITY AND EMBRACING THE OTHER

Most in the Western world cannot imagine a scenario in which they might endanger their children or trust their family to the fate of strangers in order to avoid severe persecution, torture, and execution for their faith. But that is Sarah's story. She, her husband (formerly a house church pastor in Iran), and their two sons were able to escape to Malaysia a couple of years ago before things came to such a grim impasse. Life in Malaysia has its own stresses. They face financial and political instability. They never know when the police might shake them down or when the local government might decide to ship them back home. Making ends meet from month to month when they can't legally work is also a huge strain. But they are grateful to be alive and together.

Malaysia is a major relay station on the refugee highway. Iranians are one group coming to Malaysia in large numbers. Many arrive to seek asylum with the United Nations High Commission on Refugees (UNHCR). This is a long, grueling process. They have to make an appointment to make their claim of asylum. Then they must go through a series of interviews where government, police, and military officers question them about their claims. The whole process, if it happens without any hitches, takes about three years. In the meantime they are stuck in a country in which they don't speak any of the main languages and cannot legally find employment. Unscrupulous employers force these refugees to work long hours for meager wages. They know that they could lose their jobs at any time. For those with families, they have the added pressure of trying to continue their children's education.

One of the recurring themes among refugees is the increased stress brought on by isolation in the midst of so many difficulties. They have low levels of trust for other people, especially for those from their own country. This cuts them off from any support networks they can find. What they need is warmth, compassion, and welcome—the loving hospitality of strangers.

Paul and Charis Wan are friends of ours who work with refugee groups in Malaysia. They have helped Sarah and her family find accommodation, employment, and friendship in Kuala Lumpur. The Wans try to help refugees and asylum seekers in tangible ways. But the best thing they offer is friendship, dignity, hospitality, and a listening ear. So many refugees are dealing with their trauma and stress in isolation. They need genuine friendship and emotional support. They need to know someone cares, even when support groups can't fix all their problems. Refugee life is lonely and vulnerable. Their presence among us offers a perfect opportunity for us to love our neighbors.

The UNHCR's "Global Trends 2012 Report—Displacement: The New 21st Century Challenge," which we mentioned earlier in the book, analyzes trends among refugees, asylum seekers, returnees, stateless persons, and groups of internally displaced persons (IDPs). The report estimates that in 2012 almost fifty million people were forcibly displaced worldwide. Persecution, conflict, violence, and human-rights violations caused these people to flee their homes. Developing countries hosted over 80 percent of the world's refugees. Children (those below eighteen years old) made up 50 percent of the refugee population.[16]

How should Christians respond to such need? In a word: hospitality.

But we don't just offer hospitality to refugees and migrants. We offer hospitality to all in the Spirit of Christ. Our God is a hospitable God who welcomes and embraces the other. God calls us to keep in step with the hospitable Spirit, welcoming and embracing the other too.

Throughout successive generations, all over the globe, human beings have recognized the intimate connections between humanity, cultures, and the land. We offer hospitality from our local soil, local culture, and ultimate hope. We offer hospitality *from* a particular location—our soil, our home, our place, our culture, our relationships, our eternal hope. Hospitality's location is often *the place that I love.*

Henri Nouwen writes, "Hospitality, therefore, means primarily the creation of a free space where the stranger can enter and become a friend instead of an enemy. Hospitality is not to change people, but to offer them space where change can take place."[17] We offer hospitality *from* this location and *to* this location. We welcome others *into* our location, relationships, and place. We offer hospitality *to* that soil, that ecology, that location, and those relationships. Ruth Padilla De-Borst notes that Israel's condition as God's people was "intertwined with that of the people and place where God had situated them. *In its welfare, you will find your welfare.*"[18]

Hospitality is challenging. We need the Spirit's help to welcome and embrace the other. This requires many conversions:

> Conversion from individualism to community, from autonomy to interdependence, from idolatry to true worship, from grasping to receiving, from oppressive dominion over creation to loving care of it, from indifference to passionate, prayerful action, from Western definitions of "development" to loving participation, from competition to collaboration, from protagonism to service.[19]

Hospitality involves our relationship to our home, to the earth, and to a local place. How we treat people needs to be extended to all of creation. We need to take these things seriously to be welcoming and hospitable, and to relish the diversity of God's extraordinary banquet table. As we nurture local soils, cultures, homes, and communities, we are able to offer hospitality. Our hospitality expresses itself in actions *toward* those things and *from* them.

Ruth Padilla DeBorst claims that this involves the following:

1. *Building homes and living sustainably in them.* This means making these homes a refuge for the homeless, displaced, stranger, and rural and urban poor. (The idea of homes as refuge is truly terrifying for most people—myself included.)

2. *Planting gardens, caring for creation, and food sourcing.* We must recover "our relationship to the earth in the creation-community."

3. *Cultivating families and churches that provide "fertile ground for converted covenantal relations."* We form these relationships through intimacy, simplicity, hospitality, collaboration, and inclusion.

4. *Seeking the welfare of the city.* This includes its ecology, built environment, socioeconomic elements, human connections, and marginalized persons.[20]

Hospitality is often richest in the context of *shared history* and *generous inclusion.* Such shared history with people, place, and land is not always possible. But when it is possible and valued, it can provide a remarkable environment for hospitality and inclusion. What does it mean to enrich shared history through inclusion? It means welcoming others into our lovingly nurtured homes, lands, cultures, and communities. It means recognizing the importance of shared history and the welcome of the outsider. We open up this shared history so that the outsider can become an insider. It is an intentional openness to others entering our lives.

Our hospitality needs to be free, generous, and active. John Chrysostom, the fourth-century archbishop of Constantinople (in modern-day Turkey), charges the church to *be given* to hospitality.[21]

We welcome people into our homes in hopeful anticipation of our ultimate home. In welcoming them, we welcome Jesus Christ. Quakers refer to "that of God in everyone." This reminds us that what we do to others, we do to Christ. When we welcome the least of them, we are welcoming Jesus.

Hospitality will often disappoint us. People will wound us, use us, and let us down. They will betray our trust and refuse to reciprocate in kind. Hospitality will be a "now/not yet" experience. Sometimes it will be as unpleasant as foot washing. Some will offer us hospitality in return—enriching our lives more than we could have imagined. It was like that for Jesus.

But hospitality makes us fuller, richer, more Christlike people. We welcome people into our homes and lives and lands in anticipation of the home and the age to come. In doing so we are a foretaste of our ultimate home and of the age to come in Christ Jesus.[22] The Spirit of hospitality opens our hearts to others, enables us to relish diversity, and inspires us to embrace the other.

HOSPITALITY AND LOVING OUR NEIGHBORS

Growing up in a Korean immigrant family was not easy for me (Grace). Our family immigrated to Canada when I was five years old. We were all faced with many difficulties, encountering pains and obstacles from the day of our arrival. I had to learn a new language and assimilate into an alien culture. I always felt out of place as a foreigner at school and in the larger community.

Some of my experiences were a result of an established system of racism and sexism that was rooted deep in the white American world I confronted. As a child with many shortcomings, it was nearly impenetrable. The institutionalized racism and sexism of the dominant culture seemed to oppose me from the outset. Thinking of my own childhood, of the flooding memories of utter toil, pain, and stereotyping that eventually led me to be marginalized by other children and the larger society, is saddening.

Just as we as people have grown from our own small and naive stature into a more developed self, so has the issue of institutional racism and sexism. It has manifested into something big and so strongly integrated into our culture that it often goes unnoticed. Secular society ignores the destructive realities and therefore does little to dismantle them. But it is our Christian responsibility to work at eliminating the evils polluting and weakening our society, communities, and churches. This can be achieved by recognizing these evils, when and where they occur, and then eviscerating the oppression and dismantling the patriarchy that pervade our Judeo-Christian tradition.

People of color have historically been ghettoized in the margins of society. They have been neglected, discriminated against, and stereotyped in North America, Australia, and other contexts. Pushed to the perimeters of their communities, people of color are sensitive to experiences of oppression. The wounds are raw and painful, not only from a brooding history but the present continuation of this mistreatment. The intersection of racism and sexism deepens the wounds and compounds the oppression that sidelined women of color experience.

Paris was attacked by ISIS terrorists on November 14, 2015. It was devastating; ISIS claimed responsibility for the deaths of over 130 people. Since this event, there have been many forms of xenophobia, racism, Islamophobia, and ill feeling toward Muslim minorities. Many people are now afraid of Syrian refugees, who are fleeing for the safety of both their family's and their own lives. Some Americans are now refusing to accept refugees into their states as they fear that they are terrorists. President Trump banned entry of refugees from seven predominantly Muslim countries for 120 days. All this is a reminder of past actions. The United States enacted the Chinese Exclusion Act of 1882, the first ban of any ethnic group into the United States. Chinese who were already in the United States had to carry identification at all times, making it difficult to travel. This ban was in place until 1943.

Can we continue to live in fear of those who are different from "our crowd"? How can we ignore the plight of those who are being chased out of their country and seeking refuge in a foreign country? Are we following God in all this fear, blame, and neglect of others, or are we neglecting God's commandment to love our neighbors?

In this broken world of misgivings, misrepresentations, and misunderstandings among the diverse human family created by God, Jesus revealed our need to explore the margins and create a pathway toward healing and hope. Jesus' family was in fact a refugee family who fled into Egypt as Herod ordered the slaughter of young children. By definition Jesus was in fact the other who was pushed to the margins of society. As a poor Jewish peasant teacher from Nazareth, Jesus was marginalized by the leaders in Jerusalem. He stood in solidarity with the marginalized lower classes. Jesus incarnated life, practiced kindom teaching, and was crucified on a criminal's cross, revealing God's transformative love working for justice, peace, and liberation.

The healing of divisions in this world happens through God's transformative Spirit of love. With restless hearts, we often long to connect with God, the other, and the community that is in touch with God's creation. Through the practice of prayer our longing is transformed into a Spirit of love. The Spirit gives us strength to love God and our neighbor.

As we accept our differences and work out tensions between peoples, we understand that it is the Spirit God who can bring us together. Being in connection with one another is a formative power that can strengthen our very existence. Everything that exists comes into being by virtue of connectedness. The Spirit-led life helps us to stay connected to God and each other in deep solidarity. This is especially the case as we serve together in the work of social transformation. The Spirit is the true source of restoring right relationships and enabling respect and love for others, even others who are completely different from us.

Spirit God energizes us for the work of healing in the world. Spirit God emboldens and enables us to respect and welcome the other. All people are made in the image of God, and we are called to love our neighbor just as we love ourselves. Since we are all created in the image of a God who loves us completely and eternally—no matter who we are or what we do—we are called to love all people with that same extravagant and inclusive love.

HOSPITALITY AND THE FUTURE OF THE CHURCH

As we have noted already, the world is becoming increasingly diverse. We are living in a multicultural, multiethnic, multi-everything world. Some who realize this are gripped by fear, anxiety, and longing for the past. But this global change is not to be feared or resisted. Instead this is a wonderful opportunity to show the world what redeemed and transformed humanity looks like. This is a chance to show the power of faith, welcome, hospitality, reconciliation, and hope. This is a time to fully embrace love and to welcome the dynamic, enriching life together that diversity enables. This is an opportunity to truly be the new humanity in Jesus Christ. This is a chance to reactivate hospitality so that it infuses every part of the church's witness and life together.

PRACTICES, CHALLENGES, AND ACTIVITIES FOR SMALL GROUPS

Here are some practices and activities for your small group. These will help you embrace the practice of hospitality.

Do the eight-week small group curriculum about multiethnic conversations. As a small group, read and take part in *Multiethnic Conversations: An Eight-Week Journey Toward Unity in Your Church* together.[23] This small group curriculum will help you understand the biblical principles behind diverse, multiethnic congregations. It will help you discuss race, class, culture, and church. It will help you move toward a multiethnic and multicultural future as a small group and as an entire congregation.

Consider doing a faith-based cultural intelligence (CQ) assessment.
The Cultural Intelligence Center offers faith-based cultural intelligence assessments. Here's their description:

> Religious communities are faced with many opportunities and challenges due to our increasingly diverse world. How do faith-based communities remain true to their convictions while simultaneously adjusting to and learning from those with different cultural systems and beliefs? Enhance the multicultural understanding and effectiveness of your faith-based group by assessing their cultural intelligence (CQ). Surveys include questions specifically designed to trigger reflection about religious issues and concerns in multicultural contexts. We offer the online assessments and personalized feedback reports for faith-based contexts.[24]

Listen to a selection of the GlobalChurch Project videos and/or podcasts, and use the free small group discussion guides that go with each video. The GlobalChurch Project invites often-unheard voices from around the world to enter into a powerful global conversation about the shape of church and mission in the twenty-first century. It provides a platform for multicultural, minority, indigenous, and Majority World voices. The GlobalChurch project videos and podcasts will help you see the global diversity of the church and help you learn from diverse voices from around the world. These videos will provide insight on how diversity may be the future of the church. Each video has a small group discussion guide that your group can use for free. These free videos, podcasts, and small group discussion guides will help your church and small group become more innovative, missional, and multicultural. Access the videos and podcasts at https://theglobalchurchproject.com.

SEVEN

REINFORCE AGENCY

I n 2007 **Australian Prime Minister** John Howard launched the Australian federal government intervention into remote Aboriginal communities. He did this in response to claims of rampant child sexual abuse and neglect in those communities. The "Little Children Are Sacred" report made ninety-seven recommendations for dealing with child sexual abuse and neglect in remote Aboriginal communities (of which only two were eventually implemented; in the seven years since the intervention, not one charge of child sexual abuse has been made).[1]

What did "the intervention" (as it has become known) look like? The Australian federal government seized control of seventy-three remote Aboriginal communities. More than six hundred soldiers and defense force personnel entered those communities. They enforced policing, instituted alcohol restrictions, restricted welfare, and enforced schooling among Aboriginal children. Customary law and cultural practice considerations were removed from legal proceedings. Welfare payments were restricted and rationed in a way that would be completely unacceptable to the rest of Australian society.

The intervention had its supporters and critics, both Aboriginal and non-Aboriginal. Some Aboriginal leaders supported this intervention and its efforts to protect women and children. These leaders were often based in major cities (not in remote communities). They were often involved in politics or academia. Many Aboriginal leaders rejected or criticized the intervention. These critics were often based in remote Aboriginal communities or had direct and ongoing relationships with those communities.

In 2010 a United Nations Special Rapporteur found the intervention to be racially discriminating. He said it infringed on the human rights of Aboriginal peoples. The report acknowledged the need for emergency measures to deal with problems in remote Aboriginal communities. But it criticized the measures that limited the freedoms and autonomy of Aboriginal people (including the restrictions on access to welfare payments). Aboriginal people were denied individual and collective *agency*. And they were denied agency in a way that would have been offensive and unacceptable to non-Indigenous Australians.

The main criticism of the intervention was the lack of consultation with Aboriginal people and community leaders. The "Little Children Are Sacred" report made it clear that the only way to deal with child sexual abuse and neglect in remote Aboriginal communities was to get local communities and leaders involved in coming up with and leading local initiatives. The report warned against "centralized" intervention and encouraged "localized" solutions. In other words, Aboriginal leaders and communities needed to be empowered to find local, indigenous, autonomous solutions to local problems. The only way to solve the problems was to make local Aboriginal peoples *agents* of their own destiny.

Rosalie Kunoth-Monks is an Aboriginal woman from the Northern Territory in Australia. She lives in a place called Utopia, a group of sixteen Australian desert stations. She says,

We have all been branded grog abusers and pedophiles. What have our Utopia people got from the intervention? A police station. And guess what? We are happy that we haven't had any more things imposed on us. If we are going to be passive and sit back and allow ourselves to be removed from our homelands it would be better for the government people to come out here and shoot us. Wipe us out. Black fella bashing has become part of a political football in this country. It's not fair. Give us some space. Under the intervention, we feel like we have been made separate people but we are not enemies of the dominant culture—all we want is help to grow on our own land . . . like everyone else.[2]

Not everything about the intervention was bad. Many traditional Aboriginal elders talk about the benefits that resulted. These included more health and education funding, more help for children and women in need, and more restrictions on alcohol and drugs.

But, instead of treating Aboriginal people like they were helpless victims (or nasty perpetrators) and robbing them of their autonomy and agency, the Australian government should have done the opposite. It should have asked them what they needed. It should have acknowledged the diversity among Aboriginal cultures and supported those communities as they designed culturally specific programs. It should have treated people with dignity and respect. It should have asked them to devise and implement solutions with the help of government resources and agencies. It should have *reinforced* their agency, not robbed them of it.

WHAT IS AGENCY, AND WHY IS IT IMPORTANT?

Agency is the ability and freedom to make unrestricted and independent choices. Individuals and groups need agency to be able to express themselves fully. They need agency to determine their own futures and forge their own identities. They need agency to contribute meaningfully.

Sometimes social scientists connect and compare *agency* and *structure*. If *agency* is the ability to make free, independent, and unfettered actions and choices, then *structure* is those things that restrict and influence those actions and choices. Structures include race, gender, class, ability, religion, politics, customs, economics, traditions, institutions, culture, and so on. These structures (and systems) often prevent personal and collective agency. But, when acting redemptively and for the well-being of participants, structures can also set helpful boundaries while strengthening agency.

Take Christianity, for example. Church systems, traditions, and practices can squash personal and collective agency. They can be oppressive. (Look at the way women, children, minorities, and indigenous peoples have been silenced and disenfranchised in the history of the church and also in some parts of the world in our present-day church.) But when these structures are transformed by the values and ethics of Jesus Christ, they can be liberating and empowering. Redeemed structures provide stability, security, and protection. Transformed structures offer enriching practices and traditions. They also offer the chance to express life-giving and life-affirming forms of agency.

There's a lot of debate about the relationship between agency and structure. The debate centers on which has the most influence in determining a person's or group's future. Structures will always be present. These things will always limit and influence choices and actions. But we need to help individuals and groups express as much *agency* as possible, in spite and because of *structure*. We also need to constantly reform structure. This includes evaluating structure, confronting the status quo, addressing injustices, redeeming systems, and reinforcing agency.

HOW DO PEOPLE EXPRESS AGENCY PERSONALLY, BY PROXY, AND IN GROUPS?

As a young Korean immigrant child, I (Grace) felt that I had no voice. In part it was due to my lack of English skills, but it also was due to the structures of racism and sexism that prevented me from expressing my thoughts, ideas, and understandings. The school I attended did not particularly encourage my participation and shrugged off my inactivity to "shyness." But in actuality it was because I did not possess any agency. The Korean Presbyterian church that I attended was sexist in all aspects of its worship and community. I could not speak out against this patriarchy because there was no space for such forms of criticism to be heard and welcomed. I didn't have the agency to call out racism in the school or sexism in the church.

Albert Bandura says that agency is "the human capability to exert influence over one's functioning and the course of events by one's actions. . . . Through cognitive self-guidance, humans can visualize futures that act on the present; construct, evaluate, and modify alternative courses of action to gain valued outcomes; and override environmental influences."[3] He adds, "To be an agent is to influence intentionally one's functioning and life circumstances."[4]

Bandura and Martin Hewson go further and specify that there are three kinds of agency, which overlap and integrate.[5] These are personal agency, proxy agency, and collective agency. *Personal agency* is about what people can do individually to affect what they can control directly. We exercise personal agency when we seek to directly influence, control, or change our personal circumstances. Many factors influence our ability to exercise personal agency. *Proxy agency* occurs when people invite those with more (or different) power, knowledge, means, or influence to act on their behalf. Agency by proxy happens when we seek to advocate for others and when we empower them to act. But agency by proxy happens most effectively when those people invite us to do so. *Collective agency* happens when people work as a group to bring change that benefits the whole group. We live our lives in groups. Often change and action are only possible when we work together interdependently to achieve desirable outcomes. As we combine our voices, passions, skills, networks, influence, and so on, we achieve more. This has a multiplying effect on what we can achieve—our collective voice and action is often powerful.

But here's an important point. The crucial factor in people's willingness to exercise personal or collective agency is their belief that they can make a difference. Bandura puts it this way: "Unless people believe they can produce desired effects and forestall undesired ones by their actions, they have little incentive to act or to persevere in the face of difficulties."[6] If we believe that we are powerless, then chances are we won't act. But if we believe that we can make a difference and that we can influence the course of events by our actions, then chances are we will act, often with great resolve and courage.

WHAT ROLES DO THOSE WITH POWER OR FROM THE MAJORITY CULTURE PLAY IN REINFORCING AGENCY?

We all have an important role to play in reinforcing others' agency. No matter whether we are part of a minority group or the majority culture, and no matter whether we are a man or a woman, we can all do our part to support another person or group's ability to exercise control, make decisions, act, speak, and pursue change. I (Grace), as a woman of color who lacked agency for much of my life, have often struggled with gaining power and agency. Presently, with some level of education and with a certain amount of "power" as a professor in a seminary, it is important for me to encourage others who feel powerless to be empowered and to support their agency.

If we are part of the majority culture (and thus have unique power in that setting) we have a special responsibility to fortify, support, and ensure the agency of others. This is especially true for men within the dominant culture, as men usually have gendered power within societies. White, male, educated, professional, middle-aged men, for example, have a lot of cultural power to act and influence systems and structures, especially compared with other groups. Men have a definite obligation to buttress and champion the voice and the agency of women. Those of us who are men and women from the majority culture have a distinct responsibility to reinforce and champion the voice and the agency of people from minority groups.

But how do we do this?

TRANSFORMING OUR THEOLOGY OF THE CHURCH AND OUR VISION OF A HEALTHY, MISSIONAL CHURCH

As Christians two things can help motivate us to reinforce another person's or group's agency. The first is a transformed theology of the church. The second is a renewed vision of what a healthy, missional church looks like.

God calls the church to be a unified and diverse body. God invites the church to join with him in reaching and transforming every tribe, people, ethnicity, and nation. God works in and through racial, gender, linguistic, and generational diversity. This extraordinary mosaic emerges out of God's extravagant hospitality, welcome, and love. God is reconciling the world in Jesus Christ, calling every ethnicity, and both women and men, to join in that ministry of peacemaking and reconciliation. Since all this is true, how can we not reinforce the agency and voice of others? How can we not give ourselves completely to helping others (and especially those who've been marginalized, silenced, and disempowered) to have an honored, free, loved, welcomed, and valued voice and contribution?

This yearning for new life within the church then spills over into our hope and action in the world. God loves justice. God calls his church to work for justice in the world. This includes putting our energies into helping all people in society (and especially women, minorities, the poor, the disabled, and those marginalized) to have an uninhibited and valued influence and input. Our goal, as the people of God in the world, is to help people exert influence over their lives, circumstances, societies, churches, and destinies.

Rev. Karen Hernandez-Granzen, who ministers at Westminster Presbyterian Church of Trenton in New Jersey, is engaging in missional ministry. She has a multiethnic and redemptive community church that shows the world what it looks like in its redeemed state. She prioritizes and honors the voices and contributions of women, minorities, indigenous peoples, the poor, the disabled, and those marginalized. This church is a light to a divided and broken world. By empowering and profiling the voices of those often neglected, this church witnesses to God's extravagant love and justice by breaking down the dividing walls of animosity, hatred, fear, discrimination, and exclusion.

Reinforcing agency is another way of talking about being a transformed, healthy, missional church—one that welcomes the stranger, offers good news to the broken and poor, shines in the darkness, and practices lavish welcome, hospitality, and embrace. As it welcomes, loves, and esteems the lost, the last, and the least, the church is the light of the world and a city on a hill that cannot be hidden (Mt 5:14).

EMBRACING CORPORATE PRACTICES THAT REINFORCE AGENCY (INSIDE AND OUTSIDE THE CHURCH)

Churches also need to embrace practices that reinforce people's agency (and especially women and minority groups), both inside and outside the church. What are some of these corporate practices?

- Provide occasions for minoritized and female voices and perspectives to be heard and honored. These opportunities may be in community and neighborhood settings, in small groups, or during worship services.

- Invite local people (and especially minorities and women) to fashion ministries, churches, missions, leadership practices, and services that genuinely meet the needs of their neighborhoods and cultures.

- Worship in ways that are indigenous to all the cultures and groups in your church. If you have multiple cultures and groups in your church, provide space for them to express worship, theology, and ministry in a way that makes sense to their culture. These expressions of faith should be so close to the heart of those cultures that they make sense to believers and nonbelievers alike.

- Make sure your congregation is a place where local minorities, indigenous groups, and women *take part in* and *lead* the ministries and mission of the church. Collaborate with them so that they *own* these ministries and missions and expressions of the church.

- Refuse to blindly import theologies, church models, governance structures, and worship expressions, especially those that only reflect majority cultures. Instead, empower your congregation (and especially the minorities and less vocal members of your church) to make their own decisions and determine their own programs and structures.

- Invite minorities and women to form their own theologies and shape their own ministries, while you do the same. This is another way majority and minority groups and cultures can enrich each other. This is about mutuality, equality, and sharing. It models diversity in unity.

- Ask minorities, indigenous groups, and women to help enrich your theology and biblical understandings. Throw fuel on the fire of local theological imagination. Listen to history and tradition. Respect the authority of Scripture. Pay close attention to the interpretations of people of color. Be theologically imaginative. Strive for theological innovations, interpretations, and explorations. Allow these to challenge *and* confront the majority culture and its normal way of doing theology and reading the Bible. Give fresh weight to the stories, images, ideas, and interpretations of those who are not a part of the majority culture.

- Seek to pursue diversity in unity, even when it is hard work. Honor a plurality of voices, ideas, ethnicities, skin colors, and languages. Together, as one diverse and unified body, seek to transform, animate, direct, and unify your cultures.

- Reinforce agency for all people (inside and outside the church), not only for the sake of your church or neighborhood but also for the sake of the whole world. This posture and these practices help enrich and extend the church local and global.

- When asked to speak at an event, suggest names of people of color and women who can speak too.

- Make sure that women and people of color are involved in speaking at conferences and panels and in planning those events (see chapter four on relinquishing power). Make sure they are serving in positions of power and have equal access to attending the conference and building dynamic networks.

- Work hard for diversity in whatever area of influence you have: church, politics, business, health care, education, and so on.

- Be willing to make the sacrifice of losing/sharing your role for the sake of the church hearing minority voices.

As churches, be flowerpot breakers and seed sowers. Sri Lankan preacher and evangelist Daniel Thambyrajah Niles puts it this way:

The gospel is like a seed and you have to sow it. When you sow the seed of the gospel in Palestine, a plant that can be called Palestinian Christianity grows. When you sow it in Rome, a plant of Roman Christianity grows. You sow the gospel in Great Britain and you get British Christianity. The seed of the gospel is later brought to America and a plant grows of American Christianity. Now when missionaries came to our lands they brought not only the seed of the gospel, but their own plant of Christianity, flowerpot included! So, what we have to do is to break the flowerpot, take out the seed of the gospel, sow it in our own cultural soil, and let our own version of Christianity grow.[7]

Minority, indigenous, and female voices can work together to help Christian faith flourish in their setting. Smash the flowerpot of majority culture–only faith, and nurture and water the seed of diverse, multiethnic, Christ-honoring faith. We need to honor each other, pursue diversity in unity, and reinforce each other's agency (especially the agency of those who are downtrodden, silenced, marginalized, and need to rediscover their Christ-honoring agency and power).

PRACTICES, CHALLENGES, AND ACTIVITIES FOR SMALL GROUPS

Following on from the practices we've just listed, here are some other practices and activities for your small group. These will help you embrace the practice of reinforcing agency.

Seek out marginalized and minority perspectives. Don't know where to start? Join a community group or Christian group made up from various ethnicities and genders, and listen and learn from their perspectives and experiences. Invite women, people of color, and marginalized people to present at your small group. Ask them to help you think about race and gender issues, and to help you understand faith, justice, and reconciliation better. Just listen and learn. Your small group will never be the same again.

Talk about your own prejudices. In your small group, talk honestly and openly about your prejudices, racism, sexism, and blind spots.

Don't be afraid to talk about this. It is very important to share and discuss these issues so that we can learn and grow. Pray together for the courage to change, and make commitments to do so.

Advocate for those who've been silenced or denied agency. In your group, speak up for those who have been silenced in your culture or neighborhood. Talk with church, business, political, and other leaders. Write letters. Speak at events. Demand change. Become an ally for minorities and marginalized groups. Refuse to be silent. Join a Black Lives Matter march. Go to an Asian American, African American, Native American, or Latinx church. Demand that these people have a voice and the freedom to make free and valued decisions, actions, and choices. Posting on social media isn't enough—use your privilege, time, money, and voice to demand that others are heard and are free to decide their own challenges and futures.

Get involved. Your small group or church can't do everything alone. You need to join other groups seeking to make a difference. Get involved with Black Lives Matter, Stand with Standing Rock, the American Association of University Women, the Disability Rights Network, the Association of Women's Rights in Development, and so on.

EIGHT

RECONCILE RELATIONSHIPS

A few years ago I (Graham) had the chance to visit the Tent of Nations, which is in the West Bank in the Palestinian Territories. The Tent of Nations is a family farm owned by a Palestinian Christian family. Its mission is

> to build bridges between people, and between people and the land. We bring different cultures together to develop understanding and promote respect for each other and our shared environment. To realize this mission, we run educational projects at Daher's Vineyard, our organic farm, located in the hills southwest of Bethlehem, Palestine. Our farm is a center where people from many different countries come together to learn, to share, and to build bridges of understanding and hope.[1]

Amal Nassar and her Palestinian Christian family preach nonviolence from their farm. They've been battling to hold on to their land while Israeli settlements encroach (they've owned this land in the West Bank for one hundred years). The BBC recently ran a fascinating piece on the Tent of Nations.[2] The family is a living example of the idea of peaceful resistance.

I was delighted to interview Nassar about the Tent of Nations and to record their story and vision.³ Sitting in one of the beautiful caves on their property, we talked about justice, peace, and reconciliation in Israel-Palestine. Covering the walls of the cave are paintings and words about peace and reconciliation (written in many languages). In front of the cave is a large stone that says, "We refuse to be enemies." It was a moving experience for me.

Nassar told me a story about reconciliation. A few years ago, she unexpectedly chanced on a woman jogging past her farm. The woman was an Israeli settler we'll call Maya. Maya said to Amal, "What are you doing out here, in the middle of nowhere?"

Amal replied, "This is my family farm. We've lived here for more than one hundred years."

Incredulous, Maya replied, "That's not true. No one lives here. This is empty land. Where are the houses and roads?"

"Our homes are built among the caves," replied Amal, "and all these vineyards you see are ours."

Over the next twelve months, Amal and Maya regularly met each other during Maya's morning runs. Eventually Maya agreed to come to Amal's home for lunch. Her husband strenuously objected but finally relented. Soon Amal and Maya became friends.

One day, Maya said to Amal, "It's my son's birthday soon, and I'd like to hold the birthday party on your farm, with your family." Her Israeli settler husband wasn't happy about holding this party with a Palestinian Christian family on a Palestinian farm, but he eventually agreed. Over time, the families became close. Through friendship, patience, and understanding, they had moved from enemies to friends. This is just one example of the reconciling ministry that Nassar and her family are involved in. It's a slow and relational process.

Nassar and her family cultivate positive, proactive, and peace-making approaches to life and conflict. They are peacemakers in a region filled with conflict and injustice. For decades they've opened their home and farm to Palestinians, Israelis, and people from all over the world—inviting them to embrace the message of love and reconciliation. Students, settlers, rabbis, imams, pastors, peace activists, and a host of international guests have spent time at this farm discussing pathways to nonviolence, forgiveness, and peace. Nassar and her family choose to respond to violence in positive ways. They meet violence with love, peace, forgiveness, and embrace. Committed to breaking the cycle of violence, they build bridges, not walls. They bring people together. They know that reconciliation only happens as we address issues of justice and peace. Their lives show the power of relationships for healing conflicts and for moving toward justice, forgiveness, peace, and reconciliation.

In my interview with Nassar she shared at length how her faith in Jesus sustains her in her struggle for peace and reconciliation. Reconciliation and love of enemies is a daily decision for Palestinian Christians. They do it in the power of the Spirit and by following the life and message of Jesus Christ. These Palestinian Christians are models of love and reconciliation to the whole world.

WHAT IS RECONCILIATION?

Reconciliation isn't an easy or simple process. It involves lament, repentance, and forgiveness. It requires justice, authentic partnerships, and equality. Notice that reconciliation doesn't come first. Reconciliation is only possible after lamenting the past, repenting of our complicity, seeking forgiveness, relinquishing power, restoring justice, relishing diversity, and reinforcing agency.

In *Roadmap to Reconciliation* Brenda Salter McNeil defines *reconciliation* in a helpful way. Her definition talks about the biblical and theological *foundations* of reconciliation, the various *aspects* of reconciliation, the *process* of reconciliation, the *systemic* nature of reconciliation, and the *final goal* of reconciliation. McNeil says, "Reconciliation is an ongoing spiritual process involving forgiveness, repentance and justice that restores broken relationships and systems to reflect God's original intention for all creation to flourish."[4]

Reconciliation includes *renewing authentic partnerships* and *seeking reconciled relationships*. True reconciliation needs biblical and theological foundations. It also need to pay attention to the things McNeil mentions: fostering ongoing spiritual processes, addressing systemic injustices, restoring broken relationships and systems, and seeking God's original intention and final goal for all creation.

In *The Christian Imagination* Willie James Jennings tells a story from his childhood about white Christians who were oblivious to the faith, dreams, and needs of African Americans on their very street and in their neighborhood.[5] Reconciled partnerships are about genuinely *seeing* and *hearing* and *engaging with* the other. Such partnerships require us to work through power dynamics so that these become equal, mutual, and reciprocal partnerships. Marginalized people mustn't be recipients. They must be partners.

Reconciliation means we must cultivate lament, repentance, forgiveness, justice, partnership, dignity, and equality. We must foster identification with others and determination to change. We need to take active steps toward community building. We should pursue conflict resolution, intercultural communication, and problem solving. We must relinquish destructive power dynamics.

James H. Cone says, as we mentioned earlier, "For white people to speak of reconciliation at the very moment that they are subduing every expression of black self-determination is the height of racist arrogance."[6] As Cone says, it is racist, disingenuous, and arrogant for those of us with cultural, racial, or gender-based power to speak of reconciliation without first addressing our complicity in the personal, systemic, and structural forces that subdue and oppress the self-expression, dignity, and freedom of marginalized people. This includes, for example, the disadvantage experienced by women and people of color due to the pervasiveness of white male power and privilege.

Emmanuel Katongole and Chris Rice talk about the various visions of reconciliation. Some see reconciliation as mostly being about *individual salvation* and the reconciliation between God and humanity. Others see reconciliation as an effort to recognize and *celebrate diversity* and inclusion. Others paint a picture of reconciliation that focuses on *addressing injustice* in its many forms. Others treat reconciliation as a process of *firefighting*: overcoming urgent and immediate expressions of conflict, brokenness, and division.

These are all aspects of reconciliation. True reconciliation draws all these ideas together around the reconciling nature, story, and mission of God. So, Emmanuel Katongole and Chris Rice say that the church needs to "recover reconciliation as the mission of God."[7]

WHY SHOULD WE PURSUE RECONCILIATION?

I (Graham) need to confess something. I am racist. It's taken a while for me to admit this truth, but I finally have. As a white Australian man, I've held views about other cultures and races that are shameful. I've embraced a sense of superiority and entitlement that is often well hidden but that nonetheless shapes my view of the world and of other people. My sense of superiority and my subtle racism has shaped my positive attitudes about people like me and my negative attitudes about other ethnicities and groups. This has been so even while I've mouthed words about equality, respect, and reconciliation. This has been the case even while I've denied the presence of racism in my own life or in the people and institutions around me. So I need to acknowledge that I've indulged in subtle and shameful forms of racism. In doing so I've perpetuated the injustices around me, and I've prevented justice, peace, compassion, and reconciliation. I'm slowly changing. Little by little, I'm letting go of attitudes that my white privilege has formed in me over a lifetime. This is a slow, painful process. But I'm getting there as I listen to closely to the feedback, insights, and experience of people of color and as I submit to the Spirit.

I (Grace) want to share about the racial tension between African Americans and Korean Americans, which has had some negative consequences. Asian immigration to the United States began in the mid-1800s and continued during the country's westward expansion. Asians became "cheap labor" and were viewed as a commodity. The annexation of California in 1848 opened the floodgates for Asian labor. Asians first arrived in Hawaii, and over three hundred thousand of them entered the islands between 1850 and 1920.[8]

Koreans initially did not want to immigrate to the United States, but some missionaries persuaded members of their congregations to go to Hawaii, a Christian land. As a result, an estimated 40 percent of the seven thousand emigrants who left the country between December 1902 and May 1905 were converts.[9] Christianity has played a big role in Korean immigrants' community and individual growth. They formed their own ethnic communities to worship, learn cultural heritage, and teach Korean language to their children.

African American history is vastly different from Asian American history. It began in 1619 when Africans were brought as slaves to North America to help in the production of lucrative crops such as tobacco. Slaves helped build the economy of the United States by working in the fields. By the mid-nineteenth century, growth in the abolition movement led to the Civil War (1861–1865) and eventually to the Union victory, which freed four million slaves. By the 1960s lots of work still needed to be done, which led to the civil rights movement.

There wasn't much interaction between Asian Americans and African Americans until the 1970s. As the two groups began interacting, tensions rose and led to events such as the 1992 Los Angeles riots. The riots began on April 29 after a jury acquitted four officers of using excessive force in the arrest of Rodney King. Looting, arson, and killings resulted, and more than twenty-three hundred Korean-owned businesses were burned down or looted. This incident created deep tensions between African Americans and Korean Americans, as each blamed the other. These tensions flared again in the Baltimore riots in 2015 following the arrest and death of Freddie Gray. More than forty-two Korean American businesses were looted, burned, or damaged, and many business owners had no insurance or were underinsured. The damage done against the livelihood of Korean Americans was grave, and the tension between Korean Americans and African Americans is still evident.[10]

As of now there has not been much dialogue or intentional conversation between Korean Americans and African Americans. They view each other with suspicion. We are busy having conversations with other conversation partners but have neglected this very important discussion. Dialogue needs to be opened if the two groups want to move forward and have a better relationship with each other and with the wider community.

In addition to the evidence from the world of the need for reconciliation, in 2 Corinthians 5:11-21 Paul challenges us to embrace this vision and ministry. What is our core motivation for reconciliation? "Christ's love compels us, because we are convinced that one died for all, and therefore all died. And he died for all, that those who live should no longer live for themselves but for him who died for them and was raised again" (2 Cor 5:14-15). This extravagant love, which was revealed in the life, message, and death of Jesus, and which was poured out for all peoples, compels us to pursue a ministry of reconciliation. We do this as we live for him who died for all and was resurrected for all.

We now see people in a new way, shaped by the love and reconciling work of God. Our fellow believers are new creations, and our ministry is to take this reconciling message to the world. God has reconciled humanity to Godself in Jesus Christ, and God reconciles people to each other. Notice the movements in this story. First God reconciles us to Godself. Then God reconciles us with each other and gives us the ministry of reconciliation. The order is important, as it frames our theology of reconciliation as well as our purpose and posture in reconciliation. God makes us ambassadors of his reconciliation. Through our love, forgiveness, justice, and reconciliation, we reveal the righteousness and hope of God. "All this is from God, who reconciled us to himself through Christ and gave us the ministry of reconciliation: that God was reconciling the world to himself in Christ, not counting people's sins against them. And he has committed to us the message of reconciliation. We are therefore Christ's ambassadors, as though God were making his appeal through us" (2 Cor 5:18-20).

Reconciliation happens at many levels. God reconciles humanity to Godself, but God also enables individuals, socioeconomic groups, races, and genders to reconcile, and humanity to reconcile with creation. Through this ministry of reconciliation, God shows the world what God intends the world to be.

Revelation 7:9-10 puts it well.

> There before me was a great multitude that no one could count, from every nation, tribe, people and language, standing before the throne and before the Lamb. They were wearing white robes and were holding palm branches in their hands. And they cried out in a loud voice:
>
> "Salvation belongs to our God,
>   who sits on the throne,
>   and to the Lamb."

This is a vision of a new community worshiping God. This reconciled community comes from every society, ethnicity, gender, class, nationality, language, and age, and it seeks to bring God's peace and reconciliation to the world. This is a vision of human flourishing, of peace and shalom, of forgiveness and justice, of faith, hope, and love.

Emmanuel Katongole and Chris Rice remind us that we need a Christian vision and theology of reconciliation. We need these deep roots so that our efforts to bring reconciliation reflect the person, work, and vision of Jesus Christ.

> A Christian vision of reconciliation cannot be conceived or sustained without the particular life of the God whom Christians confess, the living God of Israel who raised the crucified Jesus from the dead. The life and preaching of Jesus shape our lives distinctly in a broken world. Shaped by convictions about God, our faith and practice point us to a deeper vocation of hope, offering a vision of what the journey of reconciliation looks like in this world, where that journey leads, how people who enter that journey are transformed along the way, and how that journey relates to neighbors, strangers and enemies. . . . Christianity offers distinct gifts of seeing, speaking about, engaging and being transformed within the world and its brokenness.[11]

Katongole and Rice go on to offer ten theses that enable us to recover "reconciliation as the mission of God."[12] Reconciliation is a process and journey aimed at transforming all humanity and creation, which requires lament and memory, and which needs the church to truly be the church. Reconciliation requires a certain kind of just, courageous, and peaceable leadership. You discover this kind of leadership through the work of the Spirit, as God transforms your heart and mind. Or, as Katongole and Rice put it, "Imagination and conversion are at the heart and soul of reconciliation."[13] God wants to transform our desires, loves, and imaginations, and to fill us with a passion for reconciliation.

The mission of the church in the world is to proclaim and embody the gospel of reconciliation, which is God restoring all things and people to Godself, and reconciling people to each other and to creation. Note the mention of creation. The World Council of Churches reminds us that making peace on earth means making peace *with* the earth.[14] We Christians have neglected to work toward climate justice by reconciling with all of creation, and it is long overdue. The consequences of not reconciling with creation are consequential and disastrous. This gospel of reconciliation calls the church to be an ethical people who seek peace and justice, and that includes creation.

John W. De Gruchy speaks of reconciliation this way:

> To say that God was reconciling the world in Christ is another way of saying that God was busy restoring God's reign of justice. One implication of this understanding of the relationship between the gospel of reconciliation and justice is that, for Paul, theology and ethics are inseparably bound together. To be reconciled to God and to do justice are part and parcel of the same process. . . . Reconciled to God, the church is a multi-ethnic community, the embodiment of a new humanity. As such it is "a novel entity on the world stage" mirroring in microcosm "the hope of the world and the universe, at present divided and at odds with its creator." . . . The church is God's reconciled and reconciling community, God's new humanity, a sign and witness of God's purpose for the whole inhabited universe or *oikumene*.[15]

This type of reconciliation requires a personal and corporate change of heart. Only God can make this possible as he leads us to repentance, justice, humility, peace, community, and a transformed spirit. L. Gregory Jones and Célestin Musekura say that God enables this kind of personal and collective change and that such transformation requires "community practices for making peace."[16] Let's look now at how we practice reconciliation.

HOW DO WE PRACTICE RECONCILIATION?

So how do we move toward reconciliation? Here are some core practices that help.

1. Develop a biblical theology of reconciliation. We've unpacked some of the dimensions of this theology already in this chapter.

Before we can practice reconciliation, we need a biblical theology that undergirds and directs reconciliation. Reconciliation isn't primarily a technique, strategy, or method. We mustn't let pragmatism hijack the church's call to reconciliation.

As we mentioned above, in the final chapter of *Reconciling All Things* Katongole and Rice offer ten theses for "recovering reconciliation as the mission of God."[17] We encourage you to get this book and read through these proposals. They will help you and your church build a robust theology of reconciliation. The final section also asks you to reflect on key biblical passages.

2. Pursue the five landmarks of reconciliation. Brenda Salter McNeil says there are five primary landmarks in the process of reconciliation.[18] The first landmark is *catalytic events*, those moments when something dramatic happens that will either inspire change or encourage preservation. There are many examples. A pastor is tired of leading a church that doesn't reflect its neighborhood and diversifies the ethnic background of the leadership team. The news media highlights the appalling levels of incarceration of black or indigenous youth. A college professor refuses to comply with racist and discriminatory policies. Saul is converted in Acts 9. This list could go on. These catalytic events either drive change and force a shift, or we regress back into preservation, depending on how we respond to them.

The second landmark is *realization*. We become aware of the discrimination, inequity, lack of diversity, and injustice around us. This goes deeper than a cognitive understanding. We experience the reality of this in context and in the lives of specific people and groups.

The third is *identification*. We identify with the other. We feel empathy for their pain, suffering, and marginalization. We understand, for instance, that for many African Americans it is plain that black lives don't seem to matter. We hear these stories and we identify, forging a new identity together.

The fourth is *preparation*. We make a conscious choice to change, and we prepare carefully and thoroughly for the change needed. We know change will be difficult and thoroughgoing, so we prepare fully.

Finally, the fifth landmark is *activation*. We do justice together as we actively work for reconciliation. McNeil talks about embracing CARE: communication, advocacy, relationships, and education.

3. Embrace the practices of reconciliation. We've enjoyed reading Drew Hart, John de Gruchy, and Brenda Salter McNeil. These authors help us understand how churches and individuals can practice reconciliation.

Today the church must break its allegiance and complicity with racist ideologies, systems, and practices. How do we do that? Drew Hart recommends sharing life with another racial group, practicing solidarity with those who suffer, seeing the world from below, subverting racial hierarchies in church and society, embracing a renewed social imagination (through the power of Scripture and the Spirit), seeking first God's kingdom, and engaging in self-examination.[19]

But those aren't the only practices we need.[20] We restore justice and enable reconciliation when we create space for people to get to know others from different ethnic and cultural groups. John de Gruchy reminds us that we need to tell the truth about injustice, wrongdoing, and guilt, and to listen to the pain and fury of those who have suffered. We must learn to forgive, which can be very difficult—both the victim and the perpetrator have roles in this. We must pursue social justice, acknowledge guilt, and reconnect love, power, and justice. For too long love, power, and justice have been separated in Christian theology and in the Christian social imagination. It's time to embrace the world-transforming power of hope. God calls the church to be a sign and herald of hope—to show the world what the world looks like in its reconciled and transformed state. The church has too often embraced a racialized imagination, a range of discriminatory practices, and a "whitened Jesus."[21]

4. Practice peacemaking and nonviolence. A lot has been written on the themes of peacemaking and nonviolence. Jesus calls his church to be a nonviolent, peaceable people. "Blessed are the peacemakers, for they will be called children of God" (Mt 5:9). Peace is at the heart of the gospel. As followers of Jesus in a divided and violent world, we are committed to finding nonviolent alternatives and to learning how to make peace between individuals, within and among churches, in society, and between nations.[22]

Stanley Hauerwas says that nonviolence and peacemaking are the "hallmarks of the Christian moral life." Nonviolence "is integral to the shape of Christian convictions."[23] We root our witness in the peaceable ethic of Jesus. "Nonviolence is a sign of hope that there is an alternative to war. And that alternative is called church."[24]

In "Peacemaking: The Virtue of the Church," Hauerwas unpacks the pastoral implications of nonviolence for the church. Peacemaking is a virtue, cultivated in community. Peacemaking is crucial to moral excellence and Christian witness. Christians can't practice peacemaking in isolation. We need communities of forgiveness, peace, hospitality, and reconciliation. Christians shouldn't despair of peace in the world. Instead we are to foster a peaceable practice and imagination. We pursue the peaceable kingdom. We embrace hope in the Prince of Peace. "Peacemaking among Christians, therefore, is not simply one activity among others but rather is the very form of the church insofar as the church is the form of the one who 'is our peace.'"[25] Peacemaking isn't passive. It's the active, courageous, and public exercise of forgiveness, love, and reconciliation.[26]

Martin Luther King Jr. preached nonviolence and peacemaking. He wrote, "World peace through non-violent means is neither absurd nor unattainable. All other methods have failed. Thus we must begin anew. Non-violence is a good starting point. Those of us who believe in this method can be voices of reason, sanity and understanding amid the voices of violence, hatred and emotion."[27] Yes, we all indeed need to be voices of reason and to engage in peacemaking and non-violent acts of resistance toward justice.

PRACTICES, CHALLENGES, AND ACTIVITIES FOR SMALL GROUPS

Here are some practices and activities for your small group. These will help you explore and experience reconciled relationships.

Consider and respond to biblical passages. Reconciliation is at the heart of the gospel and of the Christian faith. Read the following passages closely as a group, and reflect on what they mean for your ministry of reconciliation: Romans 5:10-11; 11:15; 2 Corinthians 5:18-20; Ephesians 2:14-17; Colossians 1:19-22. Brainstorm ways that you can respond to these passages practically in your community and your neighborhood.

Work through Roadmap to Reconciliation. Read Brenda Salter McNeil's book *Roadmap to Reconciliation* over eight weeks. At the end of every chapter there are practical exercises for small groups. If you are a pastor, consider asking all your church's small groups to work through the book over an eight-week period.

Watch some movies and documentaries together. Natasha Sistrunk Robinson has put together a list of movies and documentaries that stimulate discussion about race, justice, and reconciliation.[28] Develop your own list. Here are the movies that we have found most insightful, provocative, and discussion generating: *Twelve Years a Slave, District 9, Hotel Rwanda, Schindler's List, Belle,* and *The Visitor.* In your small group, get together regularly for meals and to watch these and other relevant movies. Discuss what you learn from them about race, racism, justice, and reconciliation. Even better—invite friends from minority groups over for the meal and movie so they can help you discuss and decide how you'll respond to racial injustice and race relations.

NINE

RECOVER LIFE TOGETHER

What do radical discipleship and community look like? How do we recover this life together and in the world?

The Sermon on the Mount offers a profound insight into Jesus' social ethic and into his vision for discipleship and his people's life together. In Matthew 5:1-2 Jesus is surrounded by huge crowds. He climbs a beautiful hillside overlooking a large freshwater lake and delivers the longest speech recorded in the Gospels. In this beautiful setting with an exquisite view, Jesus delivers an astonishing vision of a new people who embrace a radical, world-transforming way of life in the world.

This speech is a stunning description of Jesus' vision for life, discipleship, ethics, prayer, reconciliation, hospitality, justice, and community. It includes the Beatitudes and the Lord's Prayer, and it leaves his audience (ancient and modern) shocked and uneasy. Jesus calls his church to embrace a new, radical, ethical, and alternative way of life together in the world. He fulfills and reinterprets many aspects of the old covenant and the Ten Commandments, and he soaks this vision in prayer, love, and grace.

Again, this isn't just a picture of the individual righteous life. This is a social ethic. This is a vision of a community of disciples who pursue lives together and in the world and who witness to him, to a new humanity, and to the age to come.

Philip Yancey says that in the Sermon on the Mount we see absolute ideals and absolute grace. This isn't another form of legalism but a vision of a righteous people, utterly reliant on and empowered by God's grace. This is a vision of a people who mirror in their life together the nature of God. Jesus calls his people to pursue God's ethics and morality with great enthusiasm and dedication, but also to realize that they are only able to achieve any righteousness through grace. Here's how Yancey puts it:

> The Sermon on the Mount forces us to recognize the great distance between God and us, and any attempt to reduce that distance by somehow moderating its demands misses the point altogether.... The worst tragedy would be to turn the Sermon on the Mount into another form of legalism; it should rather put an end to all legalism.... The Sermon on the Mount proves that before God we all stand on level ground: murderers and temper-throwers, adulterers and lusters, thieves and coveters.[1]

So what kind of life together in the world does Jesus call us to embrace (in complete dependence on his grace and on the power of his Spirit)? Let's walk through the Sermon on the Mount and see what kind of people Jesus calls and invites us to be.

THE BLESSED AND ETHICAL COMMUNITY (MATTHEW 5:1-12)

Jesus describes the postures, outlook, and behaviors of blessed (happy and God-pleasing) people. These people display a compelling and distinct ethic. This ethic is personal and social, and it's rooted in the character of God. The Beatitudes should move God's people to be like

God and to depend entirely on God's grace for this to be so. The Beatitudes are a kind of prologue outlining Jesus' vision for his kin-dom, church, and disciples. This way of life together in the world is then made more explicit in the rest of the Sermon on the Mount.

As our friend John Dickson says, the Beatitudes are statements of future fact.[2] Those who are poor in spirit now will receive the kin-dom now and in the future. Those who are meek now will inherit the earth now and in the future. Those who are peacemakers now will be called the children of God now and in the kin-dom. The Beatitudes speak of the "already" and "not yet" dimensions of Jesus' age to come. We live for the future age in the present because the kin-dom was inaugurated in the life, death, and resurrection of Jesus Christ. The kin-dom will bring complete peace; we seek peace now. The age to come will bring final justice; we act in justice now. The kin-dom will bring full reconciliation; we exercise the ministry of reconciliation now. The age to come will make love supreme; we love each other and our enemies now. The kin-dom will finally free the poor and oppressed; we seek their liberation now. The age to come will bring final dignity to all people, regardless of their gender, ethnicity, class, or age; we honor all people now. And so on.

But Dickson reminds us that these Beatitudes also function as commands, both to individual disciples and to the whole church. The Beatitudes say to us: this is how the people of the kin-dom should live. That is why there are such strong connections between the Beatitudes and the themes and commands of the rest of the Sermon on the Mount.

"Blessed are the poor in spirit, for theirs is the kin-dom of heaven" (Mt 5:3).[3] God is sufficient; be satisfied. When we stop relying on our own strength and stop making life about ourselves, then God reveals Godself in and through us in surprising and redemptive ways.

"Blessed are those who mourn, for they will be comforted" (Mt 5:4). God is loving and compassionate; be comforted. When we've lost things that we love and hold dear, then God offers us his embrace and comfort.

"Blessed are the meek, for they will inherit the earth" (Mt 5:5). God is good and almighty; be meek. When we trust God and are satisfied with his love, his plan, and his goodness, then we discover that God's plan for us and the world is bigger than we ever imagined.

"Blessed are those who hunger and thirst for righteousness, for they will be filled" (Mt 5:6). God is righteous; be holy. When we hunger and thirst for God, then we find that this satisfies our hopes, desires, passions, and needs.

"Blessed are the merciful, for they will be shown mercy" (Mt 5:7). God is merciful; be forgiving. When we care for others and forgive them, then we discover the depth of God's mercy and care for us.

"Blessed are the pure in heart, for they will see God" (Mt 5:8). God is holy; be pure of heart. When our hearts are right with God, then we see God and God's presence in the world.

"Blessed are the peacemakers, for they will be called children of God" (Mt 5:9). God is peace; be peacemakers. When we seek to turn conflict and division into peace and cooperation, then people see God, and they see we are God's people. Making peace on earth also means that we need to make peace with the earth, with all of creation.

"Blessed are those who are persecuted because of righteousness, for theirs is the kin-dom of heaven. Blessed are you when people insult you, persecute you and falsely say all kinds of evil against you because of me. Rejoice and be glad, because great is your reward in heaven, for in the same way they persecuted the prophets who were before you" (Mt 5:10-12). God suffers and has given us his all; be like Jesus. When we are persecuted, ridiculed, insulted, and discredited, then we know something of the suffering of Jesus, and our reward is eternal. We are part of a community of people, stretching back to the dawn of humanity, who have suffered for God and who receive an immeasurable reward.

THE DISTINCT AND LIFE-GIVING
COMMUNITY (MATTHEW 5:13-16)

Eugene Peterson puts our call to be salt, light, and a city on a hill
this way:

> Let me tell you why you are here. You're here to be salt-
> seasoning that brings out the God-flavors of this earth.... Here's
> another way to put it: You're here to be light, bringing out the
> God-colors in the world. God is not a secret to be kept. We're
> going public with this, as public as a city on a hill.... Now that
> I've put you there on a hilltop, on a light stand—shine! Keep
> open house; be generous with your lives. By opening up to
> others, you'll prompt people to open up with God, this generous
> Father in heaven. (*The Message*)

We love the image of the church being salt-seasoning that brings out
the God-flavors of this earth, light that brings out the God-colors in
the world, and an open house that shows God's extravagant welcome
and generosity.

The church has a distinct identity and a unique social ethic and
politic.[4] Narrative shapes this social ethic, polity, and community.
Story forms our life together. It shapes our mission and service in the
world. This narrative is the story of biblical Israel and the work of
Jesus Christ.[5] This is a grand, cosmic, eschatological, and trinitarian
story. It's the story of creation, of biblical Israel, of the person and
message and work of the Jewish Jesus, of Pentecost, of the formation
of a chosen people, of the redemption and restoration of all things in
Christ, and of the coming reign of God. This narrative puts Jesus at
the center of the church's theology, discipleship, community, message,
ethic, politic, mission, and more.

The church is a community we long to belong to. We need community to survive, as it is the community that nourishes us and
teaches us what it means to love. Dorothy Day reminds us the

importance of community when she writes, "We have all known the long loneliness and we have learned that the only solution is love and that love comes with community."[6]

The church is the community formed by the story of Jesus.[7] It is a diverse community, made up of every nation, tribe, people, and language, who show extraordinary unity in diversity. God calls the church to embody that unity in diversity and that story of Jesus in its social ethic, peacemaking, life together, and mission in the world.[8]

The church remembers and tells the story of Jesus Christ. It shows the world what God calls the world to be. The church does not withdraw from the world, and the church does not stand in self-righteous judgment on the world.[9] The church serves Jesus and his world.[10] We are a life-giving community. The church, sure of its unique identity, must engage fully with the world—showing the world what God destines it to be. The church witnesses to Jesus as a peaceable, virtuous, ethical, loving, just, servant, and reconciling community.[11]

The Meeting House in Toronto is one of Canada's biggest churches. It's a poignant example of a distinct and life-giving local church, a wonderful example of a church that embodies the story of Jesus. The Meeting House is part of the Brethren in Christ (BIC), which focuses on "heart-felt devotion to Jesus, the Wesleyan pursuit of personal holiness, and the Anabaptist emphasis on simplicity, peace-making, and living out the teachings of Jesus in everyday life."[12] They seek to follow Jesus through a distinct way of life together. Their churches emphasize peacemaking, simplicity, justice, and love. Here's what The Meeting House says about itself:

> Rules, Rituals, Religion—Really? We think Jesus came to show us a different way, a better way. At The Meeting House we believe that when you see Jesus without the religious baggage we've historically put around him, you'll find someone undeniably life-changing and worth following. Everything we read

about Jesus in the Bible paints a clear picture of a revolutionary and radical who intended on turning our ways of thinking upside down and inside out. Jesus wasn't interested in creating a new religious system of do's and don'ts, wrongs and rights, rites and rules. Rather, Jesus' irreligious message is that we can only find true peace and wholeness when we embrace a love-based relationship with God, others, and even our enemies. We believe that in order to truly see Jesus, grasp his message, and follow him, we need to reject the lens given to us by religion, even the Christian religion, and become a community who opens our Bibles regularly with fresh eyes and re-live the accounts of those who first followed Jesus. Join us as we do our best to discover Jesus for who he truly is.[13]

Bringing out the God-colors in the world isn't always easy. But we follow the way of Jesus and become a distinct and life-giving church as we see and love him for who he truly is.

THE RIGHTEOUS AND JUST COMMUNITY (MATTHEW 5:17-20)

Jesus doesn't abolish the law and the prophets; he fulfills them. The heavens and the earth will disappear, but God's will and purpose will last forever. But self-righteous, legalistic, religious people and communities don't inherit God's promises or please God's heart. That isn't the righteousness God wants.

The law and the prophets talk about a better and higher righteousness, a righteousness revealed in love of God and of neighbor, shown in justice, compassion, hospitality, service, mercy, and humility. God has shown us what is good and what God requires of us: "To act justly and to love mercy and to walk humbly with your God" (Mic 6:8).

How do we recover this righteousness and justice in our life together? "'Love the Lord your God with all your heart and with all your soul and with all your strength and with all your mind'; and, 'Love your neighbor as yourself'" (Lk 10:27). Love God with all your passion and desire and hopes and intelligence and time and money and priorities and dreams and aspirations and energy. And love your neighbor as yourself—especially your neighbor who comes from a different racial, cultural, religious, gender, social, linguistic, political, and/or economic background from you. Then you will be an ethical, compassionate, and humble community. Then you will be a righteous, just, and God-pleasing people.

THE RECONCILED AND RECONCILING COMMUNITY (MATTHEW 5:21-26)

Jesus challenges his disciples to take conflict and resolution seriously. God will judge those who embrace and foster anger, division, conflict, and hatred. Jesus demands that we replace conflict, sexism, classism, violence, and racism with peace, forgiveness, love, and reconciliation.

Remember that political, social, religious, racial, and gender enmity was as strong in Jesus' day as today. Jesus was speaking to a culture soaked in conflict and animosity—much like our age. Jesus says to his disciples, "You must be different!" Earlier he tells them, "Blessed are the merciful. . . . Blessed are the peacemakers" (Mt 5:7, 9).

The part of Sydney that I (Graham) live in is one of the most religiously and ethnically diverse parts of my country. I teach at Morling College. Our Morling Residential College welcomes local university students to live on our campus. We have close to one hundred students living in this residential college, and they come from thirty-four different countries. Our aim is to be a safe and welcoming place for international university students of many countries, religions, languages, and backgrounds. Additionally, 60 percent of those who live in my suburb, Epping, were born outside Australia. Close to 60 percent of the families in my suburb are bilingual. There are many religions represented in my suburb, and 36 percent of people say they have no religion. On my street alone there are new arrivals from Korea, China, Iran, Malaysia, England, Nepal, Hong Kong, Vietnam, the Philippines, and more. If I think about the houses immediately surrounding mine, there are Hindus, Muslims, Christians, Baha'i, pagans, agnostics, and atheists. My family and I are committed to bringing love, peace, and reconciliation into this diverse community. We do that by having many families from the neighborhood over for lunches and dinners (and in doing so enjoying the cuisines and cultures of the world!) and by opening our home to many children and families from the neighborhood.

As we stated in a previous chapter, without justice, hospitality, and reconciliation the church will never be the new humanity in Jesus Christ. Through God's peace and reconciliation, we can be this peaceable and reconciling people.

God has reconciled humanity to Godself in Jesus Christ, and God reconciles people to each other. Jesus says that if you are about to perform an act of worship and there remember that you are in conflict with someone else, then first go and be reconciled. Peace and reconciliation are spiritual acts of worship.

Notice again the movements in this drama: God reconciles us to Godself, and then God reconciles us with each other and gives us the ministry of reconciliation (2 Cor 5:18-20). Because Jesus' life and death were the ultimate acts of reconciliation, he calls his church to be a reconciling people in their life together and in their life in the world.

THE HOLY AND VIRTUOUS COMMUNITY (MATTHEW 5:27-37)

Here are some alarming statistics. Research shows that 46 percent of men and 16 percent of women between the ages of eighteen and thirty-nine view pornography in any given week.[14] In another study, all young men between the ages of fifteen and twenty-nine surveyed said they had viewed pornography at some time, as did the majority of young women in the same age group. The average age of a young man's first encounter with pornography is thirteen, and for a young woman it is sixteen. Eighty percent of these young men said they watched pornography weekly, while 66 percent of the young women said they watched pornography at least monthly.[15]

Sexual addictions aren't the only moral and ethical issues plaguing modern societies. Many societies struggle with corruption, including bribery, embezzlement, abuse of political and economic power, and so on. Transparency International UK offers some troubling statistics about Europe: "According to the EU Commissioner for Home Affairs an estimated €120 billion is lost to corruption each year throughout the 27 EU member states."[16] Tax cheating costs American society around $458 billion per year.[17]

So Jesus says to his people, "Be different in your life together in the world! Your hearts are easily corrupted. Guard your hearts and your lives. Live virtuous and holy lives, just as your God is holy" (Mt 5:27-37, my paraphrase). Put away lust, sexual addictions, selfishness, moral failure, marital unfaithfulness, lies, corruption, deceit, false religiosity, and manipulation. Pursue integrity and moral excellence. You can't do this in your own strength. But the grace and power of God will help you live this way personally and in your life together.

THE RELATIONAL AND ENEMY-LOVING COMMUNITY (MATTHEW 5:38-48)

Relationship is at the very heart of Christian community. Just as the Father, Son, and Spirit exist in perfect loving community, so God invites the church into this loving relationship and calls us to imitate this love. We are a people transformed by love and relationship. All our practices and habits witness to the love of the God who is love. Our mission is to join with this loving God in inviting all people and all creation into restored and transformed relationship—with God, one another, and the earth.

Catherine Mowry LaCugna says that being in this loving community means

> living from and for God, from and for others. Living Trinitarian
> faith means living as Jesus Christ lived, in *persona Christi*:
> preaching the gospel; relying totally on God; offering healing
> and reconciliation; rejecting laws, customs, conventions that
> place persons beneath rules; resisting temptation; praying con-
> stantly; eating with modern-day lepers and other outcasts; em-
> bracing the enemy and the sinner.[18]

This love is expressed most profoundly in our love for our enemies. Jesus says that when someone attacks, offends, or insults you, you should forgive them, bless them, and act graciously and generously toward them. Embrace forgiveness and nonviolence. Loving friends and the loveable is easy. Loving and forgiving enemies is a sign of discipleship and maturity. "In a word, what I'm saying is, *Grow up.* You're kin-dom subjects. Now live like it. Live out your God-created identity. Live generously and graciously toward others, the way God lives toward you" (Mt 5:48 *The Message*).

THE GENEROUS AND COMPASSIONATE COMMUNITY (MATTHEW 6:1-4)

The crowd who gathered around Jesus on the hillside to listen to him speak were a broken, marginalized, undignified, fringe, shabby group of people. But Jesus says something shocking to *this* group. The kin-dom of God is among *you*! Blessed are *you*!

Why is Jesus' church welcoming and compassionate? Why does it give to the needy? First God is generous, loving, and inclusive. Second, this church is itself a mixed bag of people. These people gather around common meals as a symbol of their common life together and of their solidarity, hope, and transformed social relationships.

Nothing shaped the theology, community, and mission of the early church more than the people at its heart. These people were women, the poor, the sick, the outcast, the powerless, and the marginalized.[19] These groups weren't just a part of the early church community, and they didn't just heavily influence the early church community. They were at the heart of the community. They shaped the theology, fellowship, service, discipleship, and mission of the early church in immense and incalculable ways.

Jesus says to these people, and to us, care deeply and practically for those in need. But don't turn it into a performance. Don't play to the crowds or seek recognition for your actions. Do it quietly and without need for recognition. Just *be* a compassionate people. Live a generous life together in the world in such a way that people *see God* and not you.

When we think about compassionate churches, we often think of the Homeless Church. The mission of the Homeless Church in San Francisco is to bring the saving, life-changing power of Jesus Christ to the hurting people in that city. They believe that there is a solution for homelessness that does not lie in just outer changes but, more importantly, in inner transformation. They believe God can bring hope to the hopeless, healing to the sick, and confidence to those who have none left. They rely not on their own strength but in the power of God to transform lives through his church.

Evan and April Prosser received the vision for the Homeless Church while Evan was pastoring in a church (with four walls!) in Orland, California. They moved out of their comfortable home, bought a motor home, and use it as a base for mission among the homeless in San Francisco. The new church is not an outreach but a church of and for the homeless, a church on the street. It's a community made up of small "pocket bodies" wherever people live. After fourteen years of ministry among the homeless of San Francisco, the buses are gone, owing to police pressure on people living in vehicles, which resulted in no more "camps" of homeless people. So, since 2009, they have met where people gather, holding services at one of the local piers and at a big intersection in their neighborhood.[20] It's a ministry supported interdenominationally and, further down the line, it will include a warehouse where worship and preaching will be constantly happening, with services such as food, showers, laundry, and shopping cart check-in available.

THE PRAYING AND HUMBLE
COMMUNITY (MATTHEW 6:5-18)

Prayer is at the heart of our life together. This prayer is simple, quiet, and unobtrusive. It doesn't seek recognition, and it's not characterized by performance or dramatic public displays of spirituality. It doesn't dazzle. It doesn't say, "Hey, look at me!" It's simple, humble, and honest. It's complemented by our personal and social commitment to love our enemies and forgive others.

In our busyness we don't want to pray or seem to find the time to pray. But we need to pray and do so continuously. In times of trouble we need to trust God and come to God in prayer. Grace writes elsewhere, "We become the children who will pray the prayer that gives us some peace and understanding. Prayer leads us to the mystery of God and we cannot fully understand God's being, will, action and mercy towards us."[21]

Jesus says to us, "This, then, is how you should pray:

'Our Father in heaven,
hallowed be your name,
your kin-dom come,
your will be done,
    on earth as it is in heaven.
Give us today our daily bread.
And forgive us our debts,
    as we also have forgiven our debtors.
And lead us not into temptation,
    but deliver us from the evil one.'" (Mt 6:9-13)

Notice that every petition and conviction in this prayer reflects the ethics of the Sermon on the Mount. This prayer is at the heart of that sermon. This prayer reminds us to live a transformed life together as God's people and to be about what God is doing in the world.

When I (Grace) was in my PhD program, one of my professors, Ovey Muhammed, asked us, "What does it mean when we pray, 'Let thy kin-dom come'?" It sounded like a trick question, so I put my head down so that he would not ask me directly. Many of us had prayed this prayer all our lives, so we were thrown off guard by this simple question about the Lord's Prayer. When no one was able to answer the professor's question he said, "When we pray, 'Let thy kin-dom come,' we are praying, 'Let *my* kin-dom go!'" After he told us, I thought, yes, that is exactly what we are praying. We all need to let go of our individual kin-doms so that we can allow God's reign to come into the world. We need to be changed so that we can open ourselves to the work of God in the world.

Jesus calls us to seek a life of prayer, worship, simplicity, commitment to God's will, forgiveness, love for enemies, dependence on God, contentment, integrity, and humility. He calls us to pursue this life together.

THE SIMPLE AND CONTENT COMMUNITY (MATTHEW 6:19-24)

Christianity's challenge isn't relating (or being relevant) to a secular and consumerist age. It's seeing how much Christianity is now secularized, consumerist, and assimilated, and then choosing to resist and to pursue another way. Walter Brueggemann says, "The crisis in the [American] church has almost nothing to do with being liberal or conservative; it has everything to do with giving up on the faith and discipline of our Christian baptism and settling for a common, generic [American] identity that is part patriotism, part consumerism, part violence, and part affluence."[22]

The world needs persons, families, and communities that show the power of simplicity and contentment. We can't be people of both light and darkness, faith and greed, love and distrust, or God and money. Our society often tempts us to long for power, lust for sex, trust in violence, believe in the nation-state, and yearn for affluence and wealth. But we can't worship two gods at once. "Either you will hate the one and love the other, or you will be devoted to the one and despise the other. You cannot serve both God and money" (Mt 6:24).

The gods of technology, media, patriotism, sex, consumerism, the stock market, violence, guns, and affluence are never satisfied. Once they have secured your worship, they demand your entire life. More and more people are giving "tithes" to the malls they worship and online shopping sites such as amazon.com rather than tithes at church. But Jesus calls us to recover a life of God and worship together. Different values and desires shape this new life together: love, simplicity, contentment, nonviolence, and membership in Jesus' kindom. This is a radical social ethic. This is a dangerous way of life together in the world. It disrupts and confronts the status quo. It's as startling and dangerous today as it was in Jesus' time.

THE TRUSTING AND DEPENDENT COMMUNITY (MATTHEW 6:25-34)

There's a lot going on in modern societies and cities that makes us anxious, stressed, and worried. Employment is uncertain. Jobs are insecure. Money is tight. Fashion is ever changing. Living arrangements are unpredictable. Housing is expensive. Work is demanding. Technology is changing. Families and relationships are under stress. Work-life balance is difficult to achieve.

It's natural and normal to feel stressed and worried about these kinds of things. Jesus understands this, or he wouldn't have addressed the issue. But here's the good news. When you're stressed, worried, and anxious about all of life's demands, God understands and offers you another way. God cares for you, loves you, takes pride in you, and looks after your needs. God wants you to be a part of a faith community that trusts and depends on God.

How do we recover a life together that heals our own anxieties (reorienting our focus so that it's on God)? How do we join with God as he forms a people who offer peace and rest to a worried world?

We need trusting and dependent communities that embrace practices of prayer, hospitality, and peacemaking. The Waiter's Union, in Brisbane, Australia, is an example of this kind of Christian community. It describes itself as "a network of residents in West End who are committed to developing a sense of community in the locality with our neighbors, including those who are marginalized, in the radical tradition of Jesus of Nazareth." The community started with two or three households twenty years ago, and there have rarely been more than twenty households at any one time during the network's journey. The Waiter's Union cultivates intentional community wherein people can support each other through the stresses and demands of life, serve their neighborhoods, and experience peace.

> Monday mornings from 6.30 to 7.30am we meet for worship, reflection, and planning for the week. Throughout the week people meet in a range of groups to nurture their souls and sustain their faith and values. . . . Sunday night from 6.30 to 8.00pm we meet for public worship with local people in the basement of St Andrew's Anglican Church. Every two weeks we have a community meal, to which everyone is invited. Every six weeks we have a small gathering for fellowship with people in the network and every six weeks we have a large gathering with people in their region who are not in their network but who need continuing support for their faith-based community work. Every six months we have a two-week live-in community orientation program that provides an intensive introduction or

re-introduction to the spiritual disciplines that are the foundation for their faith-based community work. Every twelve
months we have a camp, to give us the chance to get away and
just relax together.

This community life supports the Waiter's Union's mission and
faith-based community work.

The most intensive learning experience found within the
network is in a household dedicated to formation. Between four
and six people live in this house at any one time.... It serves as
a resource for ongoing training in community development. In
2010, groups helping Waiters explore spirituality, philosophy,
politics, lifestyle, and so on, include short-term study groups, a
reading group, a documentary group, a men's group, and
various groups focused on social justice issues.... One group of
people the network is involved in has sought to promote the
aspirations of the original inhabitants of their neighbourhood
by lobbying for permission for them to build the as-yet-unbuilt
cultural center in Musgrave Park, which is in the middle of the
neighbourhood. Another group of people the network is involved in has sought to support refugees by sponsoring their
settlement and the settlement of their families, working through
the anguish we go through as "strangers in a strange land."
Through a whole range of groups in the network we have
sought to relate to the people in their community who have
physical, intellectual, and emotional disabilities—not as clients,
nor as consumers, still less as users—but as their friends! None
of the things that any of us are doing seems that great. However,
we constantly encourage one another to remember that true
greatness is not in doing big things, but in doing little things
with a lot of love over the long haul. And that is exactly what
we are trying to do![23]

THE GRACIOUS AND WELCOMING
COMMUNITY (MATTHEW 7:1-6)

It's far too easy to criticize people, attack their views, highlight their faults, and judge their failings. At times we're tempted to adopt a holier-than-thou and pious attitude, judging others' failings while ignoring our own. Jesus says that his people should be different. We are to be a gracious and forgiving people. Our love, graciousness, and patience are a vibrant witness, especially when others sneer and scoff.

Our graciousness is complemented by our welcome and hospitality. God chooses the weak, oppressed, broken, marginalized, and excluded. The church needs to reflect and imitate God's hospitality and graciousness. God does not form the church based on an election of the privileged, religious, and powerful few. Instead the church is a diverse and hospitable people who show authentic unity in diversity. Hospitality and grace enable us to form churches that are diverse, yet unified, and that are accepting, not judging. Hospitality and grace don't dominate, exclude, and criticize others and demand conformity. They offer "a safe and welcoming space for persons to find their own sense of humanity and worth."[24]

Jesus drives this idea home in Matthew 7:12. "So, in everything, do to others what you would have them do to you, for this sums up the Law and the Prophets." This compassionate, generous, and welcoming community looks for ways to enrich their neighborhoods; welcome the foreigner and stranger; shelter and feed those in need; share their resources, lives, and homes; honor and esteem each other; and take the initiative in doing good to others.

THE BELIEVING AND GRACE-DEPENDENT
COMMUNITY (MATTHEW 7:7-12)

Recovering life together also involves discovering together the power of faith and belief. Be direct with God, and believe that he answers prayer. God wants to bless God's people, so we ask, seek, and knock (Mt 7:7) with faith and expectation.

We love the way Jesus puts this close to the end of the Sermon on the Mount. Remember, in the Sermon on the Mount we see absolute ideals and absolute grace.[25] This is a portrait of a chosen and righteous people who are totally dependent on and empowered by God's grace. There is no way that we can live this ethical, distinct, reconciling, just, peaceable, simple, enemy-loving, virtuous, generous, prayerful, hospitable, disciplined, fruitful, wise, and sure life together without the grace of God! We are utterly dependent on grace! We can only be this kind of community if God intervenes and empowers! So we must ask for God's help to live this kind of life together in the world. We ask, seek, and knock, aware of our need for grace. We approach God with faith and anticipation. Our Father gives good gifts to those who ask him!

THE TRUE AND FRUITFUL COMMUNITY (MATTHEW 7:13-23)

Discipleship is difficult. It requires sacrifice, discipline, integrity, and holding fast to the truth. As Matthew 7:13-14 says, "Enter through the narrow gate. For wide is the gate and broad is the road that leads to destruction, and many enter through it. But small is the gate and narrow the road that leads to life, and only a few find it."

Eugene Peterson puts it like this: "Don't look for shortcuts to God. The market is flooded with surefire, easygoing formulas for a successful life that can be practiced in your spare time. Don't fall for that stuff, even though crowds of people do. The way to life—to God!—is vigorous and requires total attention" (Mt 7:13-14 *The Message*).

There will be many false teachers and disciples. Many false prophets will deliver eloquent speeches, write bestselling books, offer tantalizing promises, and drip with charm and charisma. They'll appear sincere and spiritual, but they'll seek to prey on the vulnerable and offer a way of life drenched in violence, greed, lust, fear, self-ishness, egotism, and false teachings. You'll know them by their fruit and their lack of integrity. God calls us to bear good fruit, grown in righteousness, love, and peace. By our fruit we are known. Recovering life together requires sacrifice and discipline. It involves serious discipline. It entails vigilance and passion for the truth; it demands an uncompromising commitment to the Gospel of Jesus Christ. God chooses us to bear good fruit—fruit that will last (Jn 15:16).

THE WISE AND STRONG COMMUNITY (MATTHEW 7:24-29)

The Sermon on the Mount offers a stunning vision for our life together in the world. Recovering this life together is paramount. We don't need to wonder what kind of people we need to be. In the Sermon on the Mount, Jesus tells us to be a new, ethical, transformed, grace-dependent people. We are wise builders when we construct a life together around Jesus' words.

There are churches that do live out this vision of the Sermon on the Mount. River City Church in Chicago invites everyone to worship at their church. It is a multiracial, multiethnic, and socio-economically diverse church located in the Humboldt Park area on the west side of Chicago, known for its dynamic social and ethnic community. The church holds after-school programs for children and tries its best to help those in the surrounding community who are economically poor. The white senior pastor, Reverend Daniel Hill, fights against racism and understands how white privilege works to marginalize people of color. This church is living out the gospel and the Sermon on the Mount.

When we put the vision of the Sermon on the Mount into practice, and when we completely rely on the grace and power of God to make it so, we weather the storms. We are wise builders, constructing a strong, steady, and secure house. Our strength isn't in ourselves. We're conscious of our powerlessness and weakness. We don't need to fear the storms and waves—we have built our foundation on the rock.

PRACTICES, CHALLENGES, AND ACTIVITIES FOR SMALL GROUPS

Here are some practices and activities for your small group. These will help you recover life together.

Complete Baylor University's six-week series on the Sermon on the Mount. Baylor's Center for Christian Ethics has designed a useful six-week small group series on the Sermon on the Mount. It offers prayers, Scripture readings, meditations, reflections, discussion questions, and songs on the Sermon on the Mount. We encourage you to dig deeper into the Sermon on the Mount through using this six-week series.[26]

Write modern versions of the Beatitudes and the Sermon on the Mount. As a small group spend an evening writing modern versions of the Beatitudes and the Sermon on the Mount. If Jesus were delivering these today, how would he say these things? What other words would he use, and what other issues would he include? Be creative.

Recently Pope Francis proposed six new Beatitudes for modern Christians:[27]

- Blessed are those who remain faithful while enduring evils inflicted on them by others and forgive them from their heart.

- Blessed are those who look into the eyes of the abandoned and marginalized and show them their closeness.

- Blessed are those who see God in every person and strive to make others also discover him.

- Blessed are those who protect and care for our common home.

- Blessed are those who renounce their own comfort in order to help others.

- Blessed are those who pray and work for full communion between Christians.

As a small group, have a go at writing Jesus' Beatitudes in your own words. But also add some new Beatitudes that come directly out of Jesus' words in the entire Sermon on the Mount (make sure your new Beatitudes are true to the things Jesus says in Matthew 5–7).

Put the Sermon on the Mount into practice in your neighborhood. Here's a way your small group can put the Sermon on the Mount into practice in your neighborhood.

First, open chapter nine of this book, and also open to Matthew 5–7 in your Bibles. As you read through both of these in your small group, list all the ways you can put the Sermon on the Mount into practice in your local neighborhood. Make sure these things are practical. Make sure they make sense for your neighborhood and truly meet local needs.

They may be things like this:

- Help bring peace between neighbors in conflict.

- Welcome people of different races, religions, or socioeconomic backgrounds.

- Give to families and persons in need.

- Sell assets and give to the poor.

- Welcome people into your homes for meals (especially neighbors you wouldn't normally invite).

- Plant an inclusive community garden.

If you want more examples of how to do this, look at the examples on the Parish Collective website or attend an Inhabit Conference.[28]

Start putting these things into practice in your neighborhood. Meet regularly to hold each other accountable, and to offer nurture, support, and prayer.

A BENEDICTION
AND PRAYER

We've covered nine key practices in this book that work toward healing our broken humanity. These practices revitalize the church and renew the world.

The good news is that you don't need to do these practices in your own strength. The Spirit will give you what you need to engage these practices fully. Thanks to the power of Jesus working within you, you can live differently, practice these practices, and transform a dehumanized world. Be encouraged! You can make a difference! You've taken the time to read this book and reflect on the practices. You've opened your heart, mind, and life to what God wants to do in and through you. Now, by God's grace and power, you can go and live this out.

Here's our prayer for you: May the God of creation expand your heart and mind as you reimagine the church as the new humanity in Christ. May God give you endurance and encouragement as you seek to change your world, to live in harmony with one another, and with one voice to glorify God (Rom 15:5-6).

May the God of hope fill you with all joy and peace in believing, so that by the power of the Holy Spirit you may abound in hope

(Rom 15:13). May the Spirit of courage help you lament the past together, help you have the willingness to repent of white cultural captivity and the determination to confront racial and gender injustice. We pray that the Spirit would give you the strength you need to give up your privilege, self-interests, and power, and to strive to restore justice to those who have been denied justice. May God enable you to be steadfast, immovable, always abounding in the work of the Lord, knowing that in the Lord your labor is not in vain (1 Cor 15:58).

May the God of peace and love be with you as you reinforce others' agency, practice hospitality, seek restoration, pursue reconciliation, and live in peace (2 Cor 13:11). May God fill you with passion to recover life together—as a new creation and a redeemed community. May Christ dwell in your hearts through faith, rooting and grounding you in love, so that you will know the breadth and length and height and depth of this love, and be filled with all the fullness of God (Eph 3:17-19).

Be encouraged as you seek to live differently! You can live an extraordinary, Spirit-empowered life that changes the world. You can practice these nine practices and transform a dehumanized world. You can indeed make a difference and bear fruit that will last! "Now to him who is able to do immeasurably more than all that we ask or imagine, according to his power that is at work within us, to him be glory in the church and in Christ Jesus throughout all generations, for ever and ever! Amen" (Eph 3:20-21).

ACKNOWLEDGMENTS

This book draws from many relationships. The stories and ideas we share throughout this book come from our many friendships and from our diverse personal, professional, learning, and worshiping communities. *Healing Our Broken Humanity* grew out of many conversations with colleagues, family, and friends, and many experiences of churches and individuals bringing lasting hope, deep healing, and positive change in a broken world. We would like to thank Helen Lee of InterVarsity Press for encouraging us to come together to write this book. Helen's belief in us and in this book was immensely encouraging to us and was key to getting this book launched. We are especially grateful to our InterVarsity Press editor, Al Hsu, for his enthusiasm, wise advice, and constant guidance throughout the writing of this book.

We are thankful for the learning communities of which we are a part and for the space and encouragement they provide us to wrestle with these ideas and put them in practice. We are grateful for the support shown to us by our theological colleges (for Graham, Morling Theological College in Sydney, Australia; for Grace, Earlham School of Religion in Richmond, Indiana). Our deep thanks to our many colleagues and friends in these learning communities and educational institutions, who have supported us during our time of writing. Special thanks to those who have provided wonderful feedback, support, and friendship along the way. These include Michael Frost, Darrell Jackson, Karina Kreminski, David Starling, Gayle Kent, Keith Mitchell, Tim MacBride, Andrew Sloane, Rebekah Coles, Miyon

Chung, Kristen Cairns, Anthony Petterson, Ian O'Harae, Edwina Murphy, Marc Rader, and Ian Packer.

We have sought to put the ideas of this book into practice in our local church communities. Our thanks go to Thornleigh Community Baptist Church and First Presbyterian Church for loving and supporting us, and for helping us see how local churches can live into these practices with courage and hope.

We would like to thank our friends who've provided spiritual and emotional support during the writing of this book. Your encouragement and love have meant the world to us. Your friendship has enriched our lives. We are thankful to Jessie Giyou Kim, Sung Jin and Haejeong Sue Park, Ian and Libby Packer, Anton and Megan Du Toit, Ian and Carolyn Altman, Will and Erin Sessions, Darrell and Beth Johnson Jackson, Mark Koenig, Donald McKim, Joseph Cheah, and Janice Laidlaw. You have encouraged us personally and spiritually as we've written this book.

Last, we thank our families for standing with us during the writing of this book. I (Graham) am deeply grateful for my wife, Felicity. I love you. I admire your strength of character, your passion for life, and your Christian leadership. You are the strongest, most determined leader I know, and I'm in awe of your abilities and integrity. I thank my eldest daughter, Madison, for challenging me to live out my beliefs and for never being afraid to challenge my convictions, behaviors, and ideas. You also challenge me to live a balanced life, including daily gym classes. Thanks for being willing to work out at the gym with your uncoordinated, unfit father and for inspiring me to live a fuller and richer life. I thank my daughter, Grace, for inspiring me to love Jesus more fully and to live a life of prayer, integrity, and compassion. You look right into my heart and name what is going on there, long before I can put words to my feelings, struggles, and hopes. Jesus often speaks powerfully to me through your words. I thank my youngest daughter, Dakotah, for making my life so much more enjoyable and for filling my life with laughter. Our countless hours of watching movies, playing video and board games, walking in the sun, and just having great fun have enriched my life in ways I can never describe. You make me laugh so hard my sides hurt! My family has loved and supported me throughout the writing of this book and has sacrificed so much. I'm so thankful for each of you.

I (Grace) sincerely feel indebted to my husband, Perry, for standing by me in all that I do. He has been patient and kind during my time of writing and always encouraged me to carry on. His management of our children's dance, soccer, and extracurricular events kept me sane while writing this book. I am grateful to my oldest son, Theodore, for being compassionate, loving, and kind. He is focused on his bio-medical engineering studies in college, and he has already won awards and scholarships, which makes his mom's life easier, as I do not have to worry about him or his grades. His hard work and dedication to his studies have been inspirational during my time of writing. To my beautiful daughter, Elisabeth, who is always going beyond expectations to love and bring joy and happiness to all those around her. Your dedication to ballet and your outstanding performances make me so proud of who you are. You teach me to live out my faith in unexpected ways and motivate me to be the best that I can be. To my youngest, Joshua, who is a leader among his friends and peers, and has exemplified strong leadership in school and in church: you have a kind heart and show love to everyone around you. As I am a busy mom, your gracious acceptance of mommy's absence has been unconventional but most gracious and kind. Your love pushes me to be a better mom. I am so grateful to God for blessing me with such a loving and supportive family.

QUESTIONS FOR DISCUSSION AND ENGAGEMENT

As you meet in your small group, college class, ministry team, Bible study group, or with friends, or by yourself, use any or all of the following questions to stimulate conversation and to help you apply the ten practices.

CHAPTER 1: REIMAGINE CHURCH

1. The authors say, "Christ has abolished the old divisions based on culture, politics, race, religion, law, gender, social standing, and so on. 'Christ is all, and is in all' and has brought us together from every nation, language, and people as 'one new people.'" How do we get past many of the divisions in church and society and live out this new reality?

2. This new humanity in Jesus Christ "doesn't rid us of our Jewish or Gentile (or American, Korean, Australian, Chinese, Rwandan, Brazilian, Native American, etc.) cultures, identities, and unique contributions. But now our primary identity is in Christ and in that he has made us 'one new humanity' in him." How

do you feel about this? Do you agree or disagree? How do we juggle (and integrate) our personal and ethnic identity with our primary identity in Christ and as one new people?

3. Why (and how) do we often root our Christian identity in nationalism, ethnicity, partisan politics, sociopolitical-economic status, gender, and other such things? How can we change this?

4. What's most difficult about expressing or living into the full diversity of the church? What's most rewarding?

5. The authors say that we are one body, with one Messiah, one Spirit, one life, one table, one politic, one righteousness, one peace, one mission, one faith, one hope, and one love. Which of these is most difficult to understand? Which is the hardest to express in your local church? Why is it vital for the church's witness and community that it pursue this oneness?

6. What needs to change for you and your church to reimagine the church as the new humanity in Jesus Christ?

7. What steps will you take to apply this practice fully and in the long term? Think about how you can apply this practice in your life, family, small group, church, and neighborhood.

CHAPTER 2: RENEW LAMENT

1. The authors say, "Scripture teaches us that we can't move toward hope, peace, transformation, and reconciliation without going through sorrow, mourning, regret, and lament." Why do we need to lament before we can experience healing, peace, hope, and so on?

2. Does your church practice lament? Does your culture?

3. Why is lament a foreign idea to so many of us who live in Western cultures? How can we recover lament in our gathered worship and private lives?

4. What kinds of things do your church and culture need to lament?

5. Look at the nine elements of lament. Would you modify this list in some way? What would you add or change?

6. What needs to change for you and your church to renew your practice of lamenting together?

7. What steps will you take to apply this practice fully and in the long term? Think about how you can apply this practice in your life, family, small group, church, and neighborhood.

CHAPTER 3: REPENT TOGETHER

1. Why is repentance important?

2. Look at the four stages of repentance. Would you modify this list in some way? What would you add or change?

3. What does your church and culture need to repent of?

4. The authors say that we need to ask ourselves, "How have my attitudes and practices disadvantaged the elderly, Muslims, people of color, indigenous peoples, undocumented migrants or refugees, women, the poor, those with disabilities, or other groups? How have my choices and preferences and attitudes silenced and marginalized these groups? How do my political decisions compound the problem?" Discuss these questions in your group. What do you need to repent of, and how will you embrace the mind of Christ?

5. Repentance helps us welcome, embrace, and listen to those marginalized by society. Do you agree? Why or why not?

6. What needs to change for you and your church to repent of white (or other) cultural captivity, of racial and gender injustice, and of your complicity?

7. What steps will you take to apply this practice fully and in the long term? Think about how you can apply this practice in your life, family, small group, church, and neighborhood.

CHAPTER 4: RELINQUISH POWER

1. Does your culture encourage you to acquire, consume, and accumulate things instead of giving up things? What does that say about the values and priorities of your culture?

2. What do we learn about relinquishment from the way Jesus and Paul gave up power?

3. Who do you know that models this well (someone you know personally, or maybe someone you've heard or read about)?

4. What kinds of power do you and the people in your church need to give up?

5. What does it mean in practice to embrace the power of the cross and the resurrection? How do we live that out in our daily lives?

6. What needs to change for you and your church to relinquish power (including your status, control, privilege, ambition, self-interests, political leverage, personal gain, and economic influence)? What needs to change for you to use what power you have for the sake of others and in the way of the cross?

7. What steps will you take to apply this practice fully and in the long term? Think about how you can apply this practice in your life, family, small group, church, and neighborhood.

CHAPTER 5: RESTORE JUSTICE

1. Why does justice involve walking in other people's shoes?

2. What injustices are present in your neighborhood, city, and society?

3. Why is silence a form of injustice?

4. The authors say, "God is just. The biblical story is one of a just and loving God reaching out to humanity to restore justice, wholeness, healing, and redemption. The church is an alternative community. God calls this church to embrace, proclaim, embody, and practice restored justice." Why do we need a theology of justice? Why does our concern and action for justice need to be based on our understanding of God and his work in the world?

5. Look at the four steps involved in speaking and acting for justice. How do these four steps help us seek justice for the poor, for women, for minorities, for migrants, for the earth, for the sexually abused, for people of color, and more? Why do we need partnerships with other groups to achieve this justice?

6. What needs to change for you and your church to help restore justice to those who have been denied justice?

7. What steps will you take to apply this practice fully and in the long term? Think about how you can apply this practice in your life, family, small group, church, and neighborhood.

CHAPTER 6: REACTIVATE HOSPITALITY

1. In a recent book titled *The End of White Christian America*, Robert Jones explains how a seismic change is happening in American Christianity today because America is no longer a majority white nation, culturally or demographically. The fastest-growing Christian groups in America today (and in other parts of the West) are minoritized, diaspora, and immigrant groups. How does this make you feel? What challenges and opportunities arise from this change?

2. The authors quote Mark DeYmaz as saying, "In an increasingly diverse and cynical society, those without Christ view ethnically

segregated churches as if each worship its own god as expressed in its own desires and likeness. . . . If (since) the kingdom of heaven is not segregated, local churches on earth, wherever possible, should not be either." Do you agree that we need to move away from ethnically and racially segregated churches and foster diverse, multiethnic, or intercultural churches? Why or why not?

3. What is cultural intelligence (CQ)? How can your church (and your ministry team) become more culturally intelligent?

4. Diversity requires new levels of hospitality. We must welcome and embrace the foreigner, the stranger, and the other. Ruth Padilla DeBorst says that this involves four things: (1) building homes that are a refuge for the homeless, disposed, stranger, and rural and urban poor; (2) planting gardens, caring for creation, and food sourcing; (3) cultivating families and churches that embrace intimacy, simplicity, hospitality, collaboration, and inclusion; and (4) seeking the welfare of our neighborhood and our city. Do you agree? Why or why not?

5. How do diversity and inclusion make us a fuller, richer, and more Christlike people?

6. What needs to change for you and your church to reactivate hospitality (and choose to be a people of every nation, tribe, people, and tongue) while cultivating unity in diversity?

7. What steps will you take to apply this practice fully and in the long term? Think about how you can apply this practice in your life, family, small group, church, and neighborhood.

CHAPTER 7: REINFORCE AGENCY

1. Are you familiar with the term *agency*? What does it mean?

2. Why do those in power often treat minoritized or disadvantaged groups like helpless victims (or nasty perpetrators) and rob them of their autonomy and agency?

3. How do church systems, traditions, practices, and structures sometimes squash personal and collective agency?

4. Look at the list of practices under the subheading "Embracing Corporate Practices That Reinforce Agency (Inside and Outside the Church)." What would you add to these practices?

5. At the end of this chapter, the authors challenge us to be "flowerpot breakers and seed sowers." What does this mean? How can your group be flowerpot breakers and seed sowers in your setting?

6. What needs to change for you and your church to help reinforce people's agency, especially supporting marginalized and minority groups to make free, independent, and unfettered actions and choices?

7. What steps will you take to apply this practice fully and in the long term? Think about how you can apply this practice in your life, family, small group, church, and neighborhood.

CHAPTER 8: RECONCILE RELATIONSHIPS

1. Do you agree with Brenda Salter McNeil's definition of reconciliation? Would you modify it in any way?

2. One of the authors (Graham) confesses how racism has influenced his life. Are you aware of forms of racism in your own life? How have they been expressed?

3. Why is the order of the stages in reconciliation important? "First God reconciles us to Godself. Then God reconciles us with each other and gives us the ministry of reconciliation."

4. Why do we need a biblical view of reconciliation that frames our purpose and posture in reconciliation? How do we develop this biblical view of reconciliation?

5. Look at the core practices of reconciliation. What would you add to these practices? What would you change about this list of practices?

6. What needs to change for you and your church to play your part in reconciling relationships through restoring justice and seeking repentance, forgiveness, partnership, and love?

7. What steps will you take to apply this practice fully and in the long term? Think about how you can apply this practice in your life, family, small group, church, and neighborhood.

CHAPTER 9: RECOVER LIFE TOGETHER

1. What did you learn from this chapter, especially about the Beatitudes and the Sermon on the Mount?

2. Do you agree that in the Sermon on the Mount we see absolute ideals and absolute grace? Why or why not?

3. What would the church be like if we focused on the Sermon on the Mount as much as we do on Paul's writings or on the Ten Commandments?

4. Why is love for enemies such a radical ethic? How can you and your small group and church find practical ways to love your "enemies"?

5. Which part of the Sermon on the Mount struck you the most? Which parts of the Sermon on the Mount have the most radical implications for your church and life?

6. What needs to change for you and your church to recover life together as a transformed community that lives out the vision and ethics of the Sermon on the Mount?

7. What steps will you take to apply this practice fully and in the long term? Think about how you can apply this practice in your life, family, small group, church, and neighborhood.

THE NINE
TRANSFORMING
PRACTICES
ACCOUNTABILITY FORM

This **accountability form** will help you keep each other accountable as you seek to apply these nine practices. Our discipleship is enhanced when we are a part of a small group or community of believers who offer us nurture, support, friendship, and accountability.

Access and download a PDF version of this form at https://theglobal churchproject.com/accountabilityform/. Keep a copy of this form handy (in your Bible, your bag, your journal, or somewhere else close by).

Once a week, pull this form out and write some answers to the questions on the form.

Once a month, ask everyone in your group to pull their forms out, and then discuss each of the nine practices. Hold each other accountable for the commitments you make. Ask each question of yourself, and then also ask them together (e.g., "How am *I* reimagining the church, and how are *we* reimagining the church *together*?") This group accountability will help you to continue to grow and change.

RESOURCES FOR HEALING OUR BROKEN HUMANITY

Here are some books, films, and podcasts that will help you explore how churches and individuals can embrace diversity, healing, justice, and reconciliation.

BOOKS

Barber, Leroy. *Embrace: God's Radical Shalom for a Divided World.* Downers Grove, IL: InterVarsity Press, 2016.

Boesak, Allen, and Curtiss Paul DeYoung. *Radical Reconciliation: Beyond Political Pietism and Christian Quietism.* Maryknoll, NY: Orbis, 2012.

Bonhoeffer, Dietrich. *Life Together: The Classic Exploration of Christian Community.* San Francisco: HarperOne, 2009.

Cleveland, Christena. *Disunity in Christ: Uncovering the Hidden Forces That Keep Us Apart.* Downers Grove, IL: InterVarsity Press, 2013.

DeYmaz, Mark. *Building a Healthy Multi-Ethnic Church: Mandate, Commitments and Practices of a Diverse Congregation.* San Francisco: Jossey-Bass, 2007.

Harper, Lisa Sharon. *The Very Good Gospel: How Everything Wrong Can Be Made Right.* Colorado Springs: WaterBrook, 2016.

Hill, Graham. *GlobalChurch: Reshaping Our Conversations, Renewing Our Mission, Revitalizing Our Churches.* Downers Grove, IL: Inter-Varsity Press, 2016.

———. *Salt, Light, and a City: Ecclesiology for the Global Missional Community.* Vol. 1, *Western Voices.* 2nd ed. Eugene, OR: Cascade, 2017.

James, Carolyn Custis. *Half the Church: Recapturing God's Global Vision for Women.* Grand Rapids: Zondervan, 2011.

Jennings, Willie James. *The Christian Imagination: Theology and the Origins of Race.* New Haven, CT: Yale University Press, 2011.

Johnson, Todd M., and Cindy M. Wu. *Our Global Families: Christians Embracing Common Identity in a Changing World.* Grand Rapids: Baker, 2015.

Kim, Grace Ji-Sun. *Embracing the Other: The Transformative Spirit of Love.* Grand Rapids: Eerdmans, 2015.

Kim, Grace Ji-Sun, and Jann Aldredge-Clanton, eds. *Intercultural Ministry: Hope for a Changing World.* King of Prussia, PA: Judson Press, 2017.

McNeil, Brenda Salter. *Roadmap to Reconciliation: Moving Communities into Unity, Wholeness and Justice.* Downers Grove, IL: InterVarsity Press, 2015.

McNeil, Brenda Salter, and Rick Richardson. *The Heart of Racial Justice: How Soul Change Leads to Social Change.* Downers Grove, IL: Inter-Varsity Press, 2009.

Milne, Bruce. *Dynamic Diversity: The New Humanity Church for Today and Tomorrow.* Nottingham, UK: Inter-Varsity Press, 2006.

Perkins, John M. *Dream with Me: Race, Love, and the Struggle We Must Win.* Grand Rapids: Baker, 2018.

Rah, Soong-Chan. *Many Colors: Cultural Intelligence for a Changing Church.* Chicago: Moody, 2010.

———. *The Next Evangelicalism: Freeing the Church from Western Cultural Captivity.* Downers Grove, IL: InterVarsity Press, 2009.

Saxton, Jo. *More Than Enchanting: Breaking Through Barriers to Influence Your World.* Downers Grove, IL: InterVarsity Press, 2016.

Twiss, Richard. *Rescuing the Gospel from the Cowboys: A Native American Expression of the Jesus Way.* Downers Grove, IL: InterVarsity Press, 2015.

Woodley, Randy. *Living in Color: Embracing God's Passion for Ethnic Diversity.* Downers Grove, IL: InterVarsity Press, 2004.

———. *Shalom and the Community of Creation: An Indigenous Vision.* Grand Rapids: Eerdmans, 2012.

FILMED INTERVIEWS AND PODCASTS

The GlobalChurch Project invites often-unheard voices from around the world to enter into a powerful global conversation about the shape of church and mission in the twenty-first century. At the website you can access filmed interviews and podcasts with scores of minoritized, indigenous, and Majority World (sometimes called Third World) voices. Aside from films and podcasts, the website also contains resources for small groups and college classes. Visit https://theglobalchurchproject.com.

N●TES

INTR●DUCTI●N

[1]Ta-Nehisi Coates, "Letter to My Son," *The Atlantic*, July 4, 2015, www
.theatlantic.com/politics/archive/2015/07/tanehisi-coates-between
-the-world-and-me/397619.

[2]The term *minority* when applied to groups of people has often been
viewed as characterizing them negatively and as without power. In
many ways the term *minoritized* can be helpful to use rather than
minority. *Minoritized* is used to signify that certain groups in society
are made the minority even though they may actually be in the majority in the world. For example, Asians make up nearly one-third of
the world, but when they live in the United States or Australia, they
become minoritized and have less power and less representation.

[3]This description of Stanley Hauerwas's view of practices was first pub-
lished in Graham Hill, *Salt, Light, and a City: Ecclesiology for the Global
Missional Community*, vol. 1, *Western Voices*, 2nd ed. (Eugene, OR:
Cascade, 2017), 156.

[4]Stanley Hauerwas and William H. Willimon, *Resident Aliens: Life in the
Christian Colony* (Nashville: Abingdon, 2014), 164.

[5]Stanley Hauerwas, *After Christendom: How the Church Is to Behave If
Freedom, Justice, and a Christian Nation Are Bad Ideas* (Nashville:
Abingdon, 1991), 96.

[6]Stanley Hauerwas, *A Community of Character: Toward a Constructive
Christian Ethic* (Notre Dame, IN: University of Notre Dame Press, 1991), 49.

[7]Hauerwas, *After Christendom*, 101.

[8]Here and elsewhere in this book we draw on posts by Graham Hill on
The GlobalChurch Project website, www.theglobalchurchproject
.com, and on the Missio Alliance website, www.missioalliance.org.

[9]Willie James Jennings, *The Christian Imagination: Theology and the Origins of Race* (New Haven, CT: Yale University Press, 2010), 11.

CHAPTER 1: REIMAGINE CHURCH

[1]Emmanuel Katongole, *Mirror to the Church: Resurrecting Faith After Genocide in Rwanda* (Grand Rapids: Zondervan, 2009), 1.

[2]Scot McKnight, *A Fellowship of Differents: Showing the World God's Design for Life Together* (Grand Rapids: Zondervan, 2014), 21.

[3]Bruce Milne, *Dynamic Diversity: Bridging Class, Age, Race and Gender in the Church* (Downers Grove, IL: InterVarsity Press, 2007), 16.

[4]See Willie James Jennings, *The Christian Imagination: Theology and the Origins of Race* (New Haven, CT: Yale University Press, 2010).

[5]Jürgen Moltmann, *The Church in the Power of the Spirit: A Contribution to Messianic Ecclesiology* (London: SCM Press, 1977), 197-98.

[6]Ibid.

[7]Ibid., 289.

[8]Ibid., 337-38.

[9]Ibid., 361.

[10]See Graham Hill's chapter on the Spirit in his book *Salt, Light, and a City: Introducing Missional Ecclesiology* (Eugene, OR: Wipf & Stock, 2012).

[11]Ruth Padilla DeBorst, "Living Creation-Community in God's World Today," Micah Network, accessed December 7, 2017, www.micah network.org/sites/default/files/doc/library/living_creation-community _ruthpdb.pdf.

[12]See Stanley Hauerwas, *Christian Existence Today: Essays on Church, World, and Living in Between* (Eugene, OR: Wipf & Stock, 1988), chaps. 1-2.

[13]Stanley Hauerwas and William H. Willimon, *Resident Aliens: Life in the Christian Colony* (Nashville: Abingdon, 2014), 43.

[14]Sanctuary-movement resources can be found at www.sanctuary notdeportation.org.

[15]Stanley Hauerwas, *The Peaceable Kingdom: A Primer in Christian Ethics* (London: SCM Press, 1983), 101.

[16]Ibid.

[17]Ibid., 99-103.

[18]Michael Frost, *Surprise the World: The Five Habits of Highly Missional People* (Carol Stream, IL: NavPress, 2016), 21; David J. Bosch, *Believing*

in the Future: Toward a Missiology of Western Culture (Valley Forge, PA: Trinity Press International, 1995), 33.

[19]Ibid.

[20]Graham Hill first published these three small group exercises in his book *GlobalChurch: Reshaping Our Conversations, Renewing Our Mission, Revitalizing Our Churches* (Downers Grove, IL: IVP Academic, 2016), 455-56.

CHAPTER 2: RENEW LAMENT

[1]Emmanuel Katongole, *Mirror to the Church: Resurrecting Faith After Genocide in Rwanda* (Grand Rapids: Zondervan, 2009).

[2]Ibid., 163.

[3]Patricia J. Huntington, *Loneliness and Lament: A Journey to Receptivity* (Bloomington: Indiana University Press, 2009), 6.

[4]Walter Brueggemann, *The Psalms and the Life of Faith* (Minneapolis: Fortress, 1995), 102.

[5]Soong-Chan Rah, *Prophetic Lament: A Call for Justice in Troubled Times* (Downers Grove, IL: InterVarsity Press, 2015), 20.

[6]Willie James Jennings, "Is America Willing to Be Freed from Its Demons?," Religion Dispatches, July 11, 2016, http://religiondispatches .org/is-america-willing-to-be-freed-from-its-demons.

[7]Jim Wallis, *America's Original Sin: Racism, White Privilege, and the Bridge to a New America* (Grand Rapids: Brazos, 2016), 33.

[8]Soong-Chan Rah in a Facebook conversation on Brian Bakke's Facebook site on July 10, 2016, recorded here: http://praynetwork.ning.com /forum/topics/pray-4-dallas?commentId=4597820%3AComment %3A123223.

[9]See "A Lament Table Liturgy," The Practice, accessed January 10, 2018, www.practicetribe.com/a-lament-table-liturgy.

[10]See "Writing Our Own Lament," The Practice, accessed January 10, 2018, www.practicetribe.com/wp-content/uploads/2016/02/How-to -write-your-own-lament-handout-draft-2.pdf.

[11]See "A Lament Table Liturgy (PDF)," The Practice, accessed January 10, 2018, www.practicetribe.com/wp-content/uploads/2016/02/Lament -Table-Liturgy-for-WEB-PRINT-2.pdf.

CHAPTER 3: REPENT TOGETHER

[1]"Report of the Sentencing Project to the United Nations Human Rights Committee," The Sentencing Project, August 2013, http://sentencing project.org/wp-content/uploads/2015/12/Race-and-Justice-Shadow -Report-ICCPR.pdf.

[2]Ibid.

[3]Walter Brueggemann, *A Way Other than Our Own: Devotions for Lent* (Louisville: Westminster John Knox, 2017), 3.

[4]The use of *kin-dom* comes from feminist theologians who want to portray a more inclusive understanding of God's reign. God isn't a patriarchal male figure but a loving, inclusive, and genderless God who loves all God's people regardless of race, ethnicity, and gender.

[5]Kevin Quealy and Margot Sanger-Katz, "Compare These Gun Death Rates: The U.S. Is in a Different World," *New York Times*, June 14, 2016, www.nytimes.com/2016/06/14/upshot/compare-these-gun-death -rates-the-us-is-in-a-different-world.html.

[6]Grace Ji-Sun Kim, "Obama's Legacy: Success or Status Quo?," *Huffington Post*, January 16, 2017, www.huffingtonpost.com/entry/obamas -legacy-success-or-status-quo_us_587bf3a5e4b03e071c14fe29.

[7]Tim Keel, Facebook, https://web.facebook.com/timkeel, January 26, 2017. Keel is the pastor of Jacob's Well Church in Kansas City, Missouri.

[8]"Views of Trump's Executive Order on Travel Restrictions," Pew Research Center, February 16, 2017, www.people-press.org/2017/02/16/2 -views-of-trumps-executive-order-on-travel-restrictions.

[9]See J. Kameron Carter, *Race: A Theological Account* (Oxford: Oxford University Press, 2008), and Willie James Jennings, *The Christian Imagination: Theology and the Origins of Race* (New Haven, CT: Yale University Press, 2010). See books by Willie James Jennings, Soong-Chan Rah, Christena Cleveland, Grace Ji-Sun Kim, J. Kameron Carter, Drew G. I. Hart, Brenda Salter McNeil, Rick Richardson, Jim Wallis, Emmanuel Katongole, Paula Harris, and Doug Schaupp.

[10]Here we develop the key assertions of J. Kameron Carter about whiteness and Christianity in *Race: A Theological Account*.

[11]Yassir Morsi, "Framing Racism: Why SBS's #FU2Racism Doesn't Get Race Right," Australian Broadcasting Corporation, March 3, 2017, www.abc.net.au/religion/articles/2017/03/03/4630302.htm.

[12]Andrea Smith, "Unsettling the Privilege of Self-Reflexivity," in *Geographies of Privilege*, ed. France Winddance Twine and Bradley Gardener (New York: Routledge, 2013), 268.

[13]For more information see "Theological Declaration on Christian Faith and White Supremacy," accessed December 7, 2017, www.thedeclaration.net.

[14]Graham Hill, "It's Time to Stop Organizing All White Male Conferences and Panels," The GlobalChurch Project, October 14, 2016, https://theglobalchurchproject.com/refuse-participate-unless-women-poc-stage.

[15]Graham Hill, "Women are the Heartbeat of Living Faith," The GlobalChurch Project, October 25, 2016, https://theglobalchurchproject.com/women-heartbeat-living-faith.

[16]Richard Twiss, *Rescuing the Gospel from the Cowboys: A Native American Expression of the Jesus Way* (Downers Grove, IL: InterVarsity Press, 2015).

[17]J. R. R. Tolkien, *The Fellowship of the Ring* (New York: Del Rey, 1986), 113.

[18]"Global Trends 2012 Report—Displacement: The New 21st Century Challenge," UNHCR, June 19, 2013, http://unhcr.org/globaltrends june2013/.

[19]M. Daniel Carroll R., *Christians at the Border: Immigration, the Church, and the Bible* (Grand Rapids: Brazos, 2013), xxv.

[20]Madison April Hill, "Christians at the Border: A Review by Madison April Hill," The GlobalChurch Project, May 17, 2016, https://theglobalchurchproject.com/christians-border-review-madison-april-hill.

CHAPTER 4: RELINQUISH POWER

[1]Emmanuel Katongole, *Mirror to the Church: Resurrecting Faith After Genocide in Rwanda* (Grand Rapids: Zondervan, 2009), 70.

[2]Brenda Salter McNeil, *A Credible Witness: Reflections on Power, Evangelism and Race* (Downers Grove, IL: InterVarsity Press, 2008), 66.

[3]Henri J. M. Nouwen, *The Path of Power* (London: Darton, Longman and Todd, 1995), 7-8.

[4]James H. Cone, *Black Theology and Black Power* (New York: Seabury, 1969), 147.

[5]Nouwen, *Path of Power*, 17, 23.

[6]Mother Teresa, *No Greater Love* (New World Library, 1997), 21.

[7]Yassir Morsi, "Framing Racism: Why SBS's #FU2Racism Doesn't Get Race Right," Australian Broadcasting Corporation, March 3, 2017, www.abc.net.au/religion/articles/2017/03/03/4630302.htm.

[8]Grace Ji-Sun Kim, "Hybridity, Postcolonialism and Asian American Women," *Feminist Theology* 24, no. 3 (2016): 266.

[9]For a fascinating examination of the racial and religious shifts happening in America today, see Robert P. Jones, *The End of White Christian America* (New York: Simon and Schuster, 2016).

[10]Jim Wallis, *America's Original Sin: Racism, White Privilege, and the Bridge to a New America* (Grand Rapids: Brazos, 2016), 96.

[11]Stanley Hauerwas and Jonathan Tran, "A Sanctuary Politics: Being the Church in the Time of Trump," Australian Broadcasting Corporation, March 31, 2017, www.abc.net.au/religion/articles/2017/03/30/4645538.htm.

[12]Grace Ji-Sun Kim, "Women of Color in Ministry: Ending Discrimination," *Huffington Post*, August 26, 2014, www.huffingtonpost.com/grace-jisun-kim/women-of-color-in-ministry_b_5711461.html.

[13]Wikipedia puts those with a Caucasian background at 11.5 percent of the total world population, based on census data from various nations. If half of those are women, then around 6 percent of the world's population are white men (certainly less than 10 percent). See the link here, and the associated articles and data referred to in that webpage's bibliography: https://en.wikipedia.org/wiki/White_people.

[14]Graham Hill, "It's Time to Stop Organizing All White Male Panels and Conferences," The GlobalChurch Project, October 14, 2016, https://theglobalchurchproject.com/refuse-participate-unless-women-poc-stage.

[15]Sarah Coakley, *Power and Submissions: Spirituality, Philosophy and Gender* (Milton, UK: Wiley-Blackwell, 2002), 90.

CHAPTER 5: RESTORE JUSTICE

[1]Rosemary Brennan-Herrera, "I Don't Understand How Such a Place Became Normal in the Australian Psyche," *The Age*, April 10, 2017, www.theage.com.au/comment/i-dont-understand-how-such-a -place-became-normal-in-the-australian-psyche-20170410-gvh mws.html.

[2]Chris Marshall, *The Little Book of Biblical Justice: A Fresh Approach to the Bible's Teachings on Justice* (Intercourse, PA: Good Books, 1989), 49.

[3]Ibid., 49-64.

[4]Carol J. Dempsey, *Justice: A Biblical Perspective* (St. Louis: Chalice, 2008).

[5]Danielle Strickland, *Just: Imagine the Social Justice Awakening* (Milton Keynes, UK: Authentic, 2009), 24-25.

[6]Dr. Larycia Hawkins was the first black woman to receive tenure at Wheaton College, a prominent evangelical college. On December 13, 2015, she wrote a theologically complicated Facebook post about embarking on a new journey, #embodiedsolidarity, in which she would wear a hijab during Advent in solidarity with Muslims. This got a lot of attention and led to questions of academic freedom, and the college questioned her Christian beliefs. After a tough fight, Hawkins agreed to step down from her position at Wheaton College. See Ruth Graham, "The Professor Wore a Hijab in Solidarity—Then Lost Her Job," *New York Times Magazine*, October 13, 2016.

[7]John Dear, "Romero's Resurrection," *National Catholic Reporter*, March 16, 2000, www.ncronline.org/blogs/road-peace/romeros-resurrection.

[8]Kimberlé Crenshaw, "Mapping the Margins: Intersectionality, Identity Politics, and Violence Against Women of Color," *Standard Law Review* 43 (July 1991): 1241-99.

[9]Grace Ji-Sun Kim and Susan M. Shaw, "Intersectional Theology: A Prophetic Call to Change," *Huffington Post*, March 31, 2017, www .huffingtonpost.com/entry/intersectional-theology-a-prophetic -call-for-change_us_58dd823de4b0fa4c09598794.

[10]Brenda Salter McNeil, *Roadmap to Reconciliation: Moving Communities into Unity, Wholeness and Justice* (Downers Grove, IL: InterVarsity Press, 2015), 97.

[11]Ibid., 99.

[12]See "Sustainable Development Goals," UN, accessed December 7, 2017, www.un.org/sustainabledevelopment/sustainable-development-goals/#.

[13]Cornel West, *Hope of a Tightrope: Words and Wisdom* (Carlsbad, CA: Hay House, 2008), 181.

[14]Miroslav Volf, "Forgiveness, Reconciliation, and Justice," in *Forgiveness and Reconciliation: Religion, Public Policy, and Conflict Transformation*, ed. Raymond G. Helmick and Rodney L. Petersen (Philadelphia: Templeton, 2001), 47.

[15]See Miroslav Volf's whole chapter for his complete proposal, ibid., 27-49.

[16]The Justice Conference: www.thejusticeconference.com. The Beyond Festival: https://beyondfestival.com.au. Voices for Justice: www.micah australia.org/voicesforjustice.

[17]See the Christian Community Development Association's website at https://ccda.org.

[18]"Take Action!," UN, accessed December 7, 2017, www.un.org /sustainabledevelopment/takeaction.

CHAPTER 6: REACTIVATE HOSPITALITY

[1]See Parkside Baptist Church's mission statement at www.parkside church.com.au.

[2]Grace Ji-Sun Kim, *Embracing the Other: The Transformative Spirit of Love* (Grand Rapids: Eerdmans, 2015).

[3]Bruce Milne, *Dynamic Diversity: The New Humanity Church for Today and Tomorrow* (Nottingham, UK: Inter-Varsity Press, 2006), 11.

[4]Ibid., 23.

[5]Mark DeYmaz, Facebook, April 22, 2017, https://web.facebook .com/graham.joseph.gary.hill/posts/849953245145431.

[6]Mark DeYmaz, *Leading a Healthy Multi-Ethnic Church: Seven Common Challenges and How to Overcome Them* (Grand Rapids: Zondervan, 2010), 40-44.

[7]Ibid., 44-51.

[8]"Cultural Intelligence: What It Is and Why You Need It!," Cultural Intelligence Center, accessed December 7, 2017, https://culturalq.com /what-is-cq/.

[9]Majority World Christians are those in Africa, Asia, Latin America, Eastern Europe, the Caribbean, Oceania, Muslim settings, and the Middle East. We use the term *Majority World* because the majority of the world's population is in those cultures today. The majority of the church is in those cultures too.

Indigenous Christians are those from ethnic groups indigenous to a country or territory prior to colonization or occupation. This includes people groups such as the Australian Aborigines and Torres Straight Islanders, First Nations, and Native Americans.

Immigrant and *diaspora* Christians are people scattered or dispersed beyond their original lands (especially first- and second-generation immigrants rather than longer-term residents). These include Asian Americans, Latinx, and so on.

[10]This and the next several pages draw on Graham Hill, "GlobalChurch: Learning from Majority World, Indigenous and Disapora Christians," Micah Australia, January 20, 2016, www.micahaustralia.org /globalchurch_learning_from_majority_world_indigenous_and _disapora_christians.

[11]Stephen B. Bevans, Roger Schroeder, and L. J. Luzbetak, "Missiology After Bosch: Reverencing a Classic by Moving Beyond," *International Bulletin of Missionary Research* 29, no. 2 (2005): 69.

[12]Philip Jenkins, *The Next Christendom: The Coming of Global Christianity*, 3rd ed. (Oxford: Oxford University Press, 2011), 1.

[13]Lamin Sanneh (Yale Divinity School), video interview by Graham Hill, April 20, 2015, at Yale Divinity School, New Haven, Connecticut.

[14]Bevans, Schroeder, and Luzbetak, "Missiology After Bosch," 69.

[15]See Graham Hill's book *GlobalChurch: Reshaping Our Conversations, Renewing Our Mission, Revitalizing Our Church* (Downers Grove, IL: IVP Academic, 2016), 13-20.

[16]"Global Trends 2012 Report—Displacement: The New 21st Century Challenge," UNHCR, June 19, 2013, http://unhcr.org/globaltrends june2013/. There are images, press releases, video materials, graphics, and audio recordings at the site. These bullet points are taken from the report's summary. See www.unhcr.org.uk/about-us/key-facts-and -figures.html.

[17]Henri Nouwen, *Reaching Out: The Three Movements of the Spiritual Life* (New York: Doubleday, 1986), 76-77.

[18]Ruth Padilla DeBorst, "Living Creation-Community in God's World Today," *Journal of Latin American Theology* 5, no. 1 (2010): 58.

[19]Ibid., 60.

[20]Ibid., 62-69.

[21]John Chrysostom, "Homily 21 on Romans," in *Homilies on Acts of the Apostles*, ed. J. Walker and J. Sheppard, *Nicene and Post-Nicene Fathers of the Christian Church* (New York: Christian Literature Company, 1889), 505.

[22]Grace Ji-Sun Kim, "Embracing the Other and Loving Our Neighbors," *Huffington Post*, January 14, 2016, www.huffingtonpost.com/grace -jisun-kim/embracing-the-other-and-l_b_8974778.html. We draw on this article throughout this chapter.

[23]Oneya Fennell Okuwobi and Mark DeYmaz, *Multiethnic Conversations: An Eight-Week Journey Toward Unity in Your Church* (Indianapolis: Wesleyan, 2016).

[24]"Faith-Based Assessments," Cultural Intelligence Center, accessed January 11, 2018, https://culturalq.com/products-services/assess ments/cq-assessments/faith-based-assessments/.

CHAPTER 7: REINFORCE AGENCY

[1]See the full report and recommendations here: Ampe Akelyernemane Meke Mekarle, "Little Children are Sacred," Report of the Northern Territory Board of Inquiry into the Protection of Aboriginal Children from Sexual Abuse, 2007, www.inquirysaac.nt.gov.au/pdf/bipacsa _final_report.pdf.

[2]Lindsay Murdoch, "Disputed Territory," *Sydney Morning Herald*, May 21, 2011, www.smh.com.au/national/disputed-territory-20110520-1ewrz .html.

[3]Albert Bandura, "Agency," in *Encyclopedia of the Life Course and Human Development*, ed. Deborah Carr (New York: Macmillan, 2009), 8.

[4]Albert Bandura, "Toward an Agentic Theory of the Self," in *Advances in Self Research*, vol. 3, *Self-Processes, Learning, and Enabling Human Potential*, ed. Herbert March, Ronda Craven, and Dennis McInerney (Charlotte, NC: Information Age Publishing, 2008), 16.

[5]Martin Hewson, "Agency," in *Encyclopedia of Case Study Research*, ed. Albert James Mills, Gabrielle Durepos, and Elden Wiebe (Thousand Oaks, CA: SAGE, 2010), 13-17; Albert Bandura, *Self-Efficacy: The Exercise of Control* (New York: Freeman, 1997).

[6]Bandura, "Agency," 9.

[7]Quoted in Emilio Antonio Núñez, *Crisis and Hope in Latin America: An Evangelical Perspective*, rev. ed. (Pasadena, CA: William Carey, 1996), 332-33.

CHAPTER 8: RECONCILE RELATIONSHIPS

[1]"Welcome to the Tent of Nations—An Educational and Environmental Family Farm," Tent of Nations, accessed December 7, 2017, www.tent ofnations.org/about/about-us/.

[2]Daniel Silas Adamson, "The Christian Family Refusing to Give Up Its Bethlehem Hill Farm," BBC, June 18, 2014, www.bbc.com/news /magazine-27883685.

[3]Graham Hill, "Amal Nassar | The Tent of Nations | Reconciliation, Peacemaking, and Building Bridges Between People," The Global Church Project, February 21, 2016, https://theglobalchurchproject .com/video/amal-nassar-the-tent-of-nations-reconciliation-peace making-building-bridges-between-people/.

[4]Brenda Salter McNeil, *Roadmap to Reconciliation: Moving Communities into Unity, Wholeness and Justice* (Downers Grove, IL: InterVarsity Press, 2015), 22.

[5]Willie James Jennings, *The Christian Imagination: Theology and the Origins of Race* (New Haven, CT: Yale University Press), chap. 1.

[6]James H. Cone, *Black Theology and Black Power* (Maryknoll, NY: Orbis, 1997), 147.

[7]Emmanuel Katongole and Chris Rice, *Reconciling All Things: A Christian Vision for Justice, Peace and Healing* (Downers Grove, IL: InterVarsity Press, 2008), 27-38, 147-51.

[8]Eleazar S. Fernandez, "America from the Hearts of a Diasporized People," in *Realizing the America of Our Hearts: Theological Voices of Asian Americans*, ed. Fumitaka Matsuoka and Eleazar S. Fernandez (St. Louis: Chalice, 2003), 256.

[9]Sucheng Chan, *Asian Americans: An Interpretive History* (New York: Twayne, 1991), 15.

[10] Grace Ji-Sun Kim, "Remembering Our Past for a Better Future: Asian American and Pacific Islander Heritage Month," *Huffington Post*, May 25, 2016, www.huffingtonpost.com/grace-jisun-kim/remembering -our-past-for-a-better-future-asian-american-and-pacific-islander -heritage-month_b_7433806.html.

[11] Katongole and Rice, *Reconciling All Things*, 42.

[12] Ibid., 147.

[13] Ibid., 151.

[14] For more, read Grace Ji-Sun Kim, *Making Peace with the Earth: Action and Advocacy for Climate Justice* (Geneva: WCC, 2016).

[15] John W. De Gruchy, *Reconciliation: Restoring Justice* (London: SCM Press, 2002), 54-55.

[16] L. Gregory Jones and Célestin Musekura, *Forgiving as We've Been Forgiven: Community Practices for Making Peace* (Downers Grove, IL: InterVarsity Press, 2010), 1.

[17] Katongole and Rice, *Reconciling All Things*, 147-51.

[18] McNeil, *Roadmap to Reconciliation*. See an outline of this process in chap. 2.

[19] Drew G. I. Hart, *Trouble I've Seen: Changing the Way the Church Views Racism* (Harrisonburg, VA: Herald, 2016), 167-80.

[20] De Gruchy, *Reconciliation*, 147-213.

[21] Ibid., 57.

[22] "Core Convictions," The Anabaptist Network, accessed December 7, 2017, www.anabaptistnetwork.com/coreconvictions.

[23] Stanley Hauerwas, *The Peaceable Kingdom: A Primer in Christian Ethics* (Notre Dame, IN: University of Notre Dame Press, 1991), xvi.

[24] Stanley Hauerwas and Jean Vanier, *Living Gently in a Violent World: The Prophetic Witness of Weakness* (Downers Grove, IL: InterVarsity Press, 2008), 55. Also see Hauerwas's treatment of war and peace in Hauerwas, *Approaching the End: Eschatological Reflections on Church, Politics, and Life* (Grand Rapids: Eerdmans, 2013), 120-36.

[25] Stanley Hauerwas, "Peacemaking: The Virtue of the Church," in *The Hauerwas Reader*, ed. John Berkman and Michael G. Cartwright (Durham, NC: Duke University Press, 1991), 324.

[26] Ibid., 318-26. See also Scot McKnight, *One Life: Jesus Calls, We Follow* (Grand Rapids: Zondervan, 2010), 73-84.

[27]Martin Luther King Jr., "Dreams of Brighter Tomorrows," *Ebony Magazine* (March 1965).

[28]See Natasha Sistrunk Robinson, "Race Matters: Let's Go to the Movies," *A Sista's Journey* (blog), September 12, 2014, https://asistasjourney.com/2014/09/12/race-matters-lets-go-to-the-movies/, and Natasha Sistrunk Robinson, "Race Matters: Let's Go to the Movies Part II," *A Sista's Journey* (blog), September 19, 2014, https://asistasjourney.com/2014/09/19/race-matters-lets-go-to-the-movies-part-ii/.

CHAPTER 9: RECOVER LIFE TOGETHER

[1]Philip Yancey, *The Jesus I Never Knew* (Grand Rapids: Zondervan, 1995), 143-44.

[2]John Dickson is an Australian theologian and bestselling author. This paragraph and the following one summarize and riff off his thoughts on the Beatitudes, as expressed in a Facebook conversation on Michael Frost's Facebook page on July 13, 2017. See https://web.facebook.com/michaelfrost6.

[3]In quotations from the New International Version and *The Message* we have replaced *kingdom* with *kin-dom*.

[4]See Graham Hill's chapter on Stanley Hauerwas in *Salt, Light, and a City: Ecclesiology for the Global Missional Community*, vol. 1, *Western Voices*, 2nd ed. (Eugene, OR: Cascade, 2017), chap. 16.

[5]Stanley Hauerwas, *A Community of Character: Toward a Constructive Christian Social Ethic* (Notre Dame, IN: University of Notre Dame Press, 1991), 9.

[6]Dorothy Day, *The Long Loneliness* (San Francisco: HarperOne, 2009), 286.

[7]Ibid., 50-52.

[8]Stanley Hauerwas, *After Christendom* (Nashville: Abingdon, 1991), 152.

[9]Stanley Hauerwas, *The Peaceable Kingdom: A Primer in Christian Ethics* (Notre Dame, IN: University of Notre Dame Press, 1991), 101.

[10]Ibid.

[11]Ibid., 99-103.

[12]"Who We Are," The Meeting House, accessed December 7, 2016, www.themeetinghouse.com/who-we-are/about-us/our-message/.

[13]Ibid.

[14]Mark Regnerus, David Gordon, and Joseph Price, "Documenting Pornography Use in America: A Comparative Analysis of Methodological Approaches," *The Journal of Sex Research* 53, no. 7 (2016): 873-81.

[15]Megan S. C. Lim, Paul A. Agius, Elise R. Carrotte, Alyce M. Vella, and Margaret E. Hellard, "Young Australians' Use of Pornography and Associations with Sexual Risk Behaviours," *Australian and New Zealand Journal of Public Health* (2017).

[16]"Corruption Statistics," Transparency International UK, accessed January 9, 2018, www.transparency.org.uk/corruption/corruption-statistics/.

[17]Chris Matthews, "Here's How Much Tax Cheats Cost the U.S. Government a Year," *Fortune*, April 26, 2016, http://fortune.com/2016/04/29/tax-evasion-cost/.

[18]Catherine Mowry LaCugna, *God for Us: The Trinity and Christian Life* (SanFrancisco: HarperSanFrancisco, 1993), 400.

[19]Reta Halteman Finger, *Of Widows and Meals: Communal Meals in the Book of Acts* (Grand Rapids: Eerdmans, 2007), 7-11.

[20]See Homeless Church of San Francisco, accessed January 9, 2018, www.homelesschurch.org, and their Facebook page, www.facebook.com/Homeless-Church-of-San-Francisco-150735791641216/.

[21]Grace Ji-Sun Kim, "Prayer," in *What Did Jesus Ask?: Today's Christian Leaders Illuminate the Words of Christ*, ed. Elizabeth Dias (New York: Time, 2015), 179.

[22]Walter Brueggemann, *A Way Other Than Our Own: Devotions for Lent* (Louisville: Westminster John Knox, 2016), 3.

[23]Dave Andrews and Helen Beazley, eds., *Learnings: Lessons We Are Learning about Living Together* (Eugene, OR: Wipf and Stock, 2012), 15-19. See the whole book for a detailed description of the Waiter's Union and its network, training, and lessons. See also the Waiter's Union website at www.waitersunion.org.

[24]Letty Russell, *Church in the Round: Feminist Interpretation of the Church* (Louisville: Westminster John Knox, 1993), 173.

[25]Yancey, *Jesus I Never Knew*, 143-44.

[26]Baylor University's Center for Christian Ethics, "Study Guides for Sermon on the Mount," accessed January 9, 2018, www.baylor.edu/content/services/document.php/57775.pdf.

[27]Cindy Wooden, "Pope Offers New Beatitudes for Saints of a New Age," *Catholic News Service*, January 11, 2016, www.catholicnews.com /services/englishnews/2016/pope-offers-new-beatitudes-for-saints -of-a-new-age.cfm.

[28]Parish Collective, accessed January 13, 2018, http://parishcollective .org/, and Inhabit, accessed January 13, 2018, http://inhabitconference .com/.

INDEX

aboriginal, 45-46, 49, 51-52, 68, 80-82, 126-28

agency, ix, 14, 18, 66-67, 82, 96, 126-33, 135-37, 140, 175

ambition, 14, 38, 63, 76

America, vi, 7-8, 43-44, 46, 60, 69, 114, 122, 136, 143

American, Americans, 7, 11, 15, 22-23, 25, 36, 39, 41-43, 45-46, 56, 61-62, 64-65, 67-68, 70, 109, 116, 121-22, 136-37, 141, 143-44, 148, 161, 165

anger, 8, 42, 47, 65, 159

animosity, 22, 26-27, 34, 38, 65-66, 81, 133, 159

Asia, 69, 109, 114, 116

asylum, 11, 31, 38, 45-46, 69-70, 91, 117-18

Australia, 8-9, 15, 21, 46, 49, 51, 62, 69, 80, 91, 108-9, 122, 127, 159, 167, 176

beatitudes, 152-54, 172-73

belief, 84, 131, 169, 176

Bible, i, vi, 18-19, 39, 64, 93, 100-101, 105, 135, 158

broken, i-v, ix-x, 7, 9, 11, 13, 15-17, 19, 22, 24-26, 28-30, 32, 34, 36, 38, 40, 42, 44, 46, 48, 50, 52, 54, 57-60, 62, 64, 66, 68, 70, 72, 74, 78, 80, 82, 84, 86, 88, 90, 92, 94, 96, 98, 100, 102, 104, 106, 110, 112, 114, 116, 118, 120, 122-24, 128, 130, 132-34, 136, 140-42, 144, 146, 148, 150, 154, 156, 158, 160, 162, 164, 166, 168-70, 172, 174, 176

brokenness, i, 7, 29, 41, 50, 58, 105, 142, 146

change, 8-9, 18-19, 42-43, 47-48, 56-60, 67-68, 70, 73-74, 83, 88-89, 96-97, 102, 105-7, 110, 115, 119, 124, 130-31, 137, 141, 147-49, 174, 176

Christ, iii-iv, vii, 2, 9, 11-12, 14, 21-41, 44, 58-60, 62-64, 68, 71, 76, 78, 80, 83, 86-87, 89, 93, 104, 108, 110-13, 115, 118, 120-21, 124, 129, 132, 136, 140, 144-47, 154, 156-57, 160, 162-63, 171, 174-75

Christian, ii, vi, 1-6, 8, 11-15, 23-27, 39, 46, 61, 65-66, 68-69, 83-84, 104, 106, 108, 111, 114, 116, 122, 136, 138-39, 141, 143, 145-46, 149-51, 158, 161, 165, 167, 172, 177

Christianity, 6, 13, 45, 66-67, 100, 113-16, 129, 135-36, 143, 146, 165

church, i-v, ix, 3, 5-6, 8-9, 12-18, 20-29, 31-39, 41, 43, 45-46, 48, 53, 60-62, 64-68, 70, 72, 76, 79, 82-85, 87-88, 95, 97, 101-2, 105, 108-17, 120, 124-25, 129-30, 132-35, 137, 142, 146-52, 154, 156-58, 160-63, 165-67, 169, 171, 174-75, 177

colonial, colonialism, colonization, 2-6, 45, 43, 51-52, 81, 100

community, i, iii-iv, 5, 9-14, 17, 24-28, 30, 32-34, 39, 55, 57, 64, 68, 74, 85, 89, 93, 95, 97, 102, 105-6, 108-9, 111-12, 114, 117, 119-21, 123, 127, 130, 133, 136, 141, 143-45, 147, 150-53, 155-71, 173, 175, 177

compassion, 26, 30, 47, 64, 71, 94-96, 103, 105, 118, 142, 158, 177

consumerism, 61, 96, 165-66

control, 2, 13, 34, 56, 58, 60, 74, 126, 130-31

conviction, 36, 57, 72-74, 165

countercultural, 28, 33, 38, 83, 85

cultural, 13-14, 24, 26, 29, 52, 60, 78, 82, 108, 110, 112-13, 115, 125-26, 131, 136, 141, 143, 149, 159, 168, 175

desire, 15, 47, 53, 58, 60-61, 63, 70, 82, 94, 108, 159

diaspora, 15, 36, 113, 115-16

dignity, 26, 51, 68, 81, 92, 100, 118, 128, 141, 154

disciples, 1-2, 12, 79, 85, 153-54, 159, 170

discipleship, 2, 5, 11-12, 19, 23, 32, 35, 39, 59, 61, 152, 156, 162-63, 170

discrimination, 8, 26, 28, 43, 45, 56, 60, 81-82, 84-85, 88, 93, 95-96, 99-100, 105, 133, 148

diverse, iii, 5, 8, 24-26, 28, 33, 35, 50, 100, 108-17, 123-25, 132, 135-36, 157, 159-60, 169, 171, 176

diversity, i, 22, 24-25, 27, 32, 35-36, 38, 85, 88, 104, 110-15, 119, 121, 124-25, 128, 132, 134-36, 140, 142, 148, 157, 169

ecology, 119-20

educate, education, 60, 67, 78, 81, 85, 95, 97-98, 102-3, 111, 117, 128, 131, 135, 149

ethics, ii, 9, 23, 27, 32-33, 97, 150, 152-53, 156-57, 166

ethnicity, 23, 25, 39-40, 71, 78, 99, 102, 110-11, 132, 145, 154

exclusion, 8, 14, 66, 122, 133

faith, ii, 3-4, 6, 12, 15, 19, 24, 28, 34, 36-37, 39-40, 43, 46, 57, 61, 63, 67-69, 73, 78, 83-84, 94, 104, 108, 111, 117, 124-25, 134, 136, 140-41, 145-46, 151, 162, 165-70, 175

family, vii, 9, 18, 30-31, 49, 52, 68, 80, 91-92, 102, 108, 117-18, 121-23, 138-40, 160, 176

fellowship, vi, 24, 28, 68, 71-72, 163, 167

forgiveness, 14, 22, 24, 26-27, 34, 41, 57, 63, 66, 73-74, 97, 104-5, 140-41, 145, 150, 159, 162, 165

freedom, 8, 27, 44, 51, 59, 74, 84, 91, 100, 111, 115, 128, 137, 141

friendship, vii, 54, 71, 118, 139, 177

generosity, 11, 31, 156

genocide, 41-42, 45

global church, 69, 114, 125

greed, 29, 34, 38, 56, 63, 166, 171

healing, i-v, x, 6, 22, 24, 26, 28-30, 32, 34, 36, 38, 40, 42-44, 46-48, 50, 52, 54, 58-60, 62, 64, 66, 68, 70, 72, 74, 78-80, 82, 84, 86, 88, 90, 92, 94, 96-98, 100, 102, 104, 106, 110, 112, 114, 116, 118, 120, 122-24, 128, 130, 132, 134, 136, 140, 142, 144, 146, 148, 150, 154, 156, 158, 160, 162-64, 166, 168, 170, 172, 174, 176

heaven, i, 35, 37, 112, 154-56, 164

homeless, homelessness, 45, 98, 120, 163

honor, 26, 34, 37-38, 60, 63, 135-36, 154, 169

hospitality, ix, 5, 11, 14, 24-25, 30-31, 38, 54, 70, 82, 93-94, 108-11, 113, 115, 117-21, 123-25, 132-33, 150, 152, 158, 160, 167, 169, 175

identity, 4, 8, 22-24, 33, 41, 61, 67, 100, 115, 148, 156-57, 162, 165

idolatry, 29-30, 45, 47, 60, 119

imagination, 12-13, 26-27, 66, 83, 110, 134, 141, 146, 149-50

immigrant, immigrants, 8, 15, 31-32, 36, 38, 46, 53, 67-68, 70, 75, 94, 100, 113, 116, 121, 129, 143

immigration, 31, 69, 92, 109-10, 143

indigenous, i, 2, 4, 15, 36, 39, 45, 51-52, 67-68, 71, 95, 97, 102, 113, 115-16, 125, 127, 129, 133-34, 136, 148

individualism, 11, 30, 64, 119

inequality, 43, 75, 100, 107

injustice, iii, 8, 14, 16, 21, 26, 42-44, 53, 57, 93, 95-102, 105-7, 139, 142, 148-49, 151, 175

institutional, 57, 93, 102, 121

intercultural, 24-26, 112, 141

Islam, 32

Islamophobia, 45-46, 122

Israel, 23, 36, 47, 62, 96, 119, 139, 146, 156

justice, i-iii, ix, 3, 5, 11, 14-17, 20, 24, 26-27, 29, 34, 43-44, 49, 53, 56-57, 74, 79, 82, 85, 91-107, 110, 123, 132-33, 136, 139-42, 145-47, 149, 151-52, 154, 157-58, 160, 168, 175

Korea, 30-31, 62, 84, 109, 160

Korean, 16, 22, 39, 70, 92, 121, 129-30, 143-44

lament, ii-iii, ix, 14, 24, 41-49, 51-55, 57, 72-73, 97, 140-41, 146, 175

leadership, 109, 113, 133, 146, 148, 177

liberation, 29, 99, 101, 123, 154

Malaysia, 117-18, 160
marginalized, 13, 16, 26, 46, 48, 64, 71-72, 75, 78-79, 82, 87, 94, 96, 116, 120-21, 123, 132-33, 136-37, 141, 162-63, 167, 169, 172
mission, ii, 17, 24-25, 28-29, 33, 35-36, 39, 93, 108-11, 113-14, 116-17, 125, 134, 138, 142, 146, 148, 156-57, 161-63, 168
multicultural, 35, 79, 109, 113, 124-25
multiethnic, 12, 25, 27, 35, 109, 112-13, 116, 124, 133, 136, 171
nationalism, iii, 7-8, 12, 23, 32, 45, 61, 68
neighbor, 61, 94-95, 123-24, 158-59
neighborhood, 18, 20, 30-31, 38-39, 89, 95, 102-3, 106, 133, 135, 137, 141, 148, 151, 160, 164, 173
oppression, 43, 45, 99-101, 122
Palestine, 96, 135, 138-39
peacemaking, 11, 14, 22, 34-35, 132, 139, 150-51, 157, 167
Pentecost, 25, 156
persecution, 16, 37, 69, 111, 117-18
politics, iii, 4, 8, 12, 22-23, 32, 36, 58, 60, 62, 67, 72, 127, 129, 135, 168
pornography, 160-61
poverty, 8, 36, 45, 96-97, 103, 107
power, ii-iii, ix, 1-6, 8-10, 13-14, 28-29, 33, 36-37, 43, 45, 47, 56, 58, 60, 63, 66-67, 73-74, 76-90, 93, 96, 100, 102, 115, 123-24, 130-31, 135-36, 140-41,

149, 153, 161, 163, 166, 169, 171, 174-75
privilege, 14, 45, 60, 76, 80-83, 96, 137, 141-42, 171, 175
prophetic, 48, 96, 98-99
prophets, 28, 93, 155, 158, 169-70
racism, iii, 7-8, 15, 27, 34, 38, 43, 45-48, 50, 56-57, 59-60, 66-68, 70, 74, 82-83, 96-97, 99-100, 104, 110, 121-22, 130, 136, 142, 151, 159, 171
reconciliation, i, iii, 11, 14-17, 20, 22, 24-25, 27-29, 32, 34-35, 41-42, 44, 48, 53, 57-60, 66, 70, 74, 79, 85, 95, 97, 101-5, 110, 124, 132, 136, 139-42, 144-52, 154, 159-60, 162, 175
redemption, 24, 27, 34, 97, 101, 156
refugee, 38, 69, 91-92, 104, 117-18, 123
relationship, 31, 58-59, 64, 94, 119-20, 129, 144, 147, 158, 161
relationships, ix, 14, 25, 31, 38, 53, 58-59, 74, 76, 79, 112-13, 119-20, 123, 127, 138-41, 143, 145, 147, 149, 151, 162, 166, 176
religion, ii, 8, 15, 22, 60, 62, 65, 67, 71-72, 84, 100, 114, 129, 157-58, 160, 176
renew, ii, ix, 14, 41, 43, 45, 47, 49, 51-53, 55, 117, 174
repent, ix, 14, 33, 47, 56-63, 65-75, 83, 97, 104, 175
repentance, iii-iv, 3, 5, 14, 25, 41, 43-44, 47, 53, 56-59, 70-74, 83, 85, 110, 140-41, 147

restore, ix, 14, 52-53, 82, 91, 93, 95, 97, 99, 101, 103, 105, 107, 149, 175
resurrection, 22, 27, 29, 37, 41, 78, 85-86, 154
righteous, 34, 93, 153, 155, 157-59, 170
righteousness, 14, 24, 34, 39, 57, 76-78, 95, 101, 111, 145, 153, 155, 158, 171
sexism, 15, 34, 38, 43, 45, 47, 56-57, 59-60, 66-68, 70, 75, 85, 96-97, 99, 104, 110, 121-22, 130, 136, 159
Spirit, 1-2, 5-6, 18, 24-25, 28-29, 33, 37-40, 42, 50, 53, 71-73, 79-80, 86-87, 94, 111-13, 115, 118-19, 121, 123-24, 140, 142, 146-47, 149, 153-54, 161, 174-75
spirituality, 164, 168
suffering, 37, 42-45, 47-48, 51, 70, 95, 97-98, 106, 148, 155
superiority, 13, 52, 142
supernatural, 25, 111
supremacy, iii, 5-6, 68
thanksgiving, 42-43, 48, 66
theologies, 40, 66, 97, 100, 116-17, 134
theology, i-ii, iv, 3, 15, 24-25, 35, 66, 84, 88, 100, 105, 114-16, 132, 134-35, 145, 147-49, 156, 162-63
tradition, 7, 93, 122, 134, 167
transformation, ii, 13, 35, 42, 46, 48, 123, 147, 163
tribal, 5, 8, 41
tribe, tribes, 23, 26, 29, 37, 62, 110, 132, 145, 157
Trinitarian, 156, 162

unity, 14, 17, 22, 24-27, 29-30, 34, 38, 44, 64, 66, 111-12, 124, 134-36, 157, 169

Vietnam, 16, 31, 160

violence, 2, 5, 7, 33, 44-46, 49, 61-63, 69, 80, 82, 91, 93, 105, 118, 140, 150, 159, 165-66, 171

virtue, virtuous, 33, 123, 150, 157, 160-61, 170

visions, 89-90, 142

vulnerability, vulnerable, 70, 77, 80, 89-90, 103, 118, 170

welfare, 38-39, 119-120, 126-27

worldview, worldviews, 64, 66, 110

worship, 25-26, 30, 39, 46, 54, 58-60, 73, 105, 108, 110-12, 114, 117, 119, 130, 133-34, 143, 160, 164-67, 171

youth, 52, 108-9, 148

ABOUT THE AUTHORS

GRACE JI-SUN KIM

Grace Ji-Sun Kim received her PhD from the University of Toronto and is an associate professor of theology at Earlham School of Religion. She is the author or editor of fourteen books. Her most recent publications include *Planetary Solidarity: Mother Daughter Speak*; *Intercultural Ministry*; *Making Peace with the Earth*; *Embracing the Other*; *Here I Am*; and *Christian Doctrines for Global Gender Justice*.

Grace is a series editor with Joseph Cheah for the Palgrave Macmillan series Asian Christianity in the Diaspora. She is on the American Academy of Religion's board of directors as an at-large director. She is also a cochair of AAR's Women of Color Scholarship, Teaching and Activism Group and a steering committee member of the Religion and Migration Group.

Grace writes for *Sojourners*, EthicsDaily.com, Wabash Center, and *Feminist Studies in Religion* (coeditor). She has also written for *Time*, *The Feminist Wire*, *Feminism and Religion*, *The Forum for Theological Education*, and *The Nation*. Kim is an ordained Presbyterian Church (USA) minister. More of her writing can be found on her blog, https://gracejisunkim.wordpress.com.

Grace writes in the areas of racism, sexism, climate change, and pneumatology. She is married to Perry and has three children, Theodore, Elisabeth, and Joshua.

GRAHAM HILL

Graham Hill teaches applied theology and world Christianity at Morling Theological College in Sydney, Australia. He is the founding director of The GlobalChurch Project.

Graham's website, https://theglobalchurchproject.com, contains resources to help Christian leaders and organizations thrive and grow by becoming more innovative, missional, and multicultural. His website also offers filmed interviews and podcasts with Christian leaders from all over the globe.

Graham is the author or editor of six books. His latest two are *GlobalChurch: Reshaping Our Conversations, Renewing Our Mission, Revitalizing Our Churches* (InterVarsity Press, 2016) and *Salt, Light, and a City: Ecclesiology for the Global Missional Community*, volume 1, *Western Voices*, 2nd edition (Cascade, 2017).

Graham has been in Christian ministry since 1987. He is a seasoned church planter, pastor, college professor, and church consultant. Graham did his PhD at Flinders University in Australia. He is a regular keynote speaker at conferences, churches, and colleges. Graham is passionate about world Christianity, cultural intelligence, leadership, mission, and church revitalization. This passion comes from thirty years of ministry.

Graham researches, films, and writes about trends and shifts in world Christianity. He travels all over the globe for the GlobalChurch Project, interviewing and filming Christian leaders and communities. His filmed interviews and podcasts especially focus on multicultural, minority, indigenous, and Majority World (sometimes called Third World) voices. He is married to Felicity and has three daughters, Madison, Grace, and Dakotah.